Break Through the Noise

BREAK THROUGH THE NOISE

The Nine Rules to Capture Global Attention

TIM STAPLES
and Josh Young

Houghton Mifflin Harcourt   BOSTON   NEW YORK   2019

For information about permission to reproduce selections from this book, write to trade.permissions@hmhco.com or to Permissions, Houghton Mifflin Harcourt Publishing Company, 3 Park Avenue, 19th Floor, New York, New York 10016.

hmhco.com

Library of Congress Cataloging-in-Publication Data
Names: Staples, Tim (Marketing consultant), author. |
Young, Josh (Joshua D.), author.
Title: Break through the noise : the nine rules to capture global attention / Tim Staples and Josh Young.
Description: Boston : Houghton Mifflin Harcourt, [2019] | Includes index. |
Identifiers: LCCN 2018052171 (print) | LCCN 2018055028 (ebook) |
ISBN 9781328618603 (ebook) | ISBN 9781328618566 (hardcover)
Subjects: LCSH: Internet advertising. | Internet videos. | Viral marketing. | Internet marketing.
Classification: LCC HF6146.I58 (ebook) | LCC HF6146.I58 S73 2019 (print) |
DDC 658.8/72 — dc23
LC record available at https://lccn.loc.gov/2018052171

Printed in the United States of America
DOC 10 9 8 7 6 5 4 3 2 1

"Curiosity" and "Shareability" from *The American Heritage Dictionary,*
Fifth Edition. Copyright © 2012 by Houghton Mifflin Harcourt
Publishing Company. All rights reserved.

CONTENTS

Introduction

Nobody Cares

Nobody cares.

It's very important that you understand this.

Nobody cares about that video you just posted, that photo you Instagrammed last night, and especially not that commercial that your brand just pushed out.

Really, nobody cares.

It's nothing personal. It's just the hard truth — with the explosion of social and digital media, millions of posts are launched every day. People are so bombarded by messaging that they tune out nearly all of it. So no matter how well-intentioned or beautifully designed your message is, it's destined to be lost in an avalanche of noise, chaos, and distraction. This is the reality of the internet world.

But viewers *can* be made to care. There *is* a way for major brands, small businesses, and even individuals to break through this wall of indifference and to make all the dominant social platforms — Google, Facebook, YouTube, and Instagram — work for them. The secret to making people care lies in understanding and tapping into basic human emotions and in mastering the dynamics of how to tell stories on the internet.

The process for doing this is not theoretical. Not at all. In fact, it's a practical, usable approach, based on what actually works. You can find your place in the online storytelling revolution that is blowing up the $190 billion advertising industry and altering the media land-scape.

But first, an introduction. My company, Shareability (http://www.shareability.com), is a content and marketing firm that has cracked the code of how to break through the noise of the internet and get people to not only watch content, but share it — a highly powerful concept. Our wildly popular, typically offbeat videos are far more than just fodder for Likes. They are relatable stories designed to trigger the human urge to immediately share them with their friends, friends of their friends, and people they want to have as friends.

What marketers have always known is that the most reliable way of selling something is also the most difficult to tap: *word of mouth*. Studies show that roughly 90 percent of people trust recommendations from family and friends, making the personal recommendation the elixir of marketing. For years, conventional marketing wisdom held that word of mouth was not scalable. Because of the rapid advances in technology and social media, that is no longer true. Through the way our company creates and distributes content, we have effectively figured out how to scale word of mouth.

Here are a few numbers to show that our process works. Our videos have had over 5 *billion* organic views and 50 million shares, and have generated more than 100,000 articles for major brands like Pepsi, Adobe, Hyatt, and the Olympic Games. Many brands dream of catching "lightning in a bottle" and creating just one viral hit, yet we have done it over and over and have rebuffed all of the naysayers along the way.

The interesting part is that, at their core, these videos are in fact marketing tools for brands small, medium, and large looking to find new customers and entice those customers to take action. By producing and distributing videos and posts that have maximum organic shareability, the Shareability team has tapped into a way to use

Facebook and other social media platforms to push out our videos at a fraction of the cost that most major brands typically pay.

The sharing of content online is now the single most effective way for brands to create meaningful relationships with their customers. Creating the most valuable content and building the most engaged community around that content can be worth thousands of views for some, millions of dollars for others. Today, creating this content and building a relationship with that community are cheaper and more effective than ever before — provided you understand how online storytelling actually works.

Sounds great, but what if you don't have a large marketing staff or deep-pocketed investors willing to let you experiment and learn? That's not a problem. I didn't have any of those things when I started out either.

The reality is that you can still achieve success because there are universal principles that apply to building and pushing out your brand, whatever size it may be. You don't need to know the latest and millionth change to the Facebook algorithm, because the fact is, tactical stuff in the online world doesn't age well. Rather, you need to know the philosophy of why social platforms like Facebook were founded, how they work, and how they can work for you.

This book isn't about which 84 buttons you push to cross-post on Facebook or how to hack the YouTube algorithm to make your video go viral. Rather, it's focused on understandable concepts. Hacks change every day. Concepts don't, and these are the ones that drove our business three years ago and will also work three years from now. You can't be chasing the digital breadcrumbs of every nuance and change on the major platforms.

So, that's the straightforward stuff. Of course, there is plenty that is more complex. We are going to dive deep into the current dynamics of the internet and reveal ways to ensure your messaging breaks through the noise and chaos. Using the Nine Rules that are covered in the book, we will teach you how to master the powerful concept of shareability, what you need to know about the psychology behind why people share what they do, and ultimately how to use valuable content to launch a global brand at a fraction of the cost of traditional advertising.

By understanding these Nine Rules and adapting them to your message or your brand, you can make the internet work for you, rather than fighting your way through the electronic weeds. And any message — whether it's from a community activist, a singer, or someone sitting at home with an offbeat idea that just might work — can be heard and seen by millions of people.

In short, this is a book for anyone who seeks to understand how to reach millions of people and to build an engaged and powerful brand. So whether you are an individual at a laptop trying to be heard, an entrepreneur courting investors, a small business owner trying to build your customer base, a YouTube star in the making, or the chief marketing officer for a *Fortune* 500 company, understanding and executing the Nine Rules of Shareability will help you break through the noise and take your brand further than you thought possible — and not be left to the worst fate of all: finding out that nobody cares.

Rule 1

Be Shareable

'd blown it.

I was standing outside a hotel suite in the middle of winter in Madrid, and sweat was pouring down my face. On the other side of the door was Cristiano Ronaldo, the global soccer superstar and one of the most famous people in the world.

And he had just kicked me out.

My mind raced. Today was supposed to be one of the biggest days of my career, but it was quickly becoming my worst. As I sat in the dark hallway with the sounds of a loud conversation in Portuguese pouring through the door, only one thought was blazing through my head: had we pushed it too far?

The year was 2015 and my company, Shareability, had already been behind some of the biggest viral hits of the past few years. With each new video, we had pushed the limits further and further, which gained us international attention and eventually led to meeting Ronaldo's team and getting into business with him to launch a new brand.

Hence, we were in Madrid for our first shoot with Ronaldo and his headphone brand, ROC. True to form, we were pushing the limits. Instead of merely shooting a routine commercial, we had sold him and his team on a crazy, real-world stunt, where we would dress him up as a homeless man and have him beg for money in the middle of one of the busiest plazas in Spain. A plaza, mind you, that — because of his instant recognizability — he couldn't normally walk into because he would be mobbed. Most superstars with Ronaldo's level of fame wouldn't dare such a stunt, but Ronaldo's manager, a brilliant guy named Ricardo, understands what it takes to make his friend and client stand out from the crowd of celebrities.

But when Ronaldo arrived on set, something changed. Maybe it was seeing the stony faces of the six ex-Mossad agents that we had hired to secure the plaza in the event something went wrong. Or maybe he was just having a bad day. But for whatever reason, he was now having serious second thoughts about the whole thing, and I was stuck in a hallway, struggling to keep my composure as I wiped my forehead every eight seconds.

This went on for several minutes that felt like hours. Then finally, the door swung open, and the man known around the world as CR7 stepped out. He looked at me, gave me a simple thumbs-up, and headed down the hall to wardrobe.

The shoot was on.

The resulting video, "Ronaldo in Disguise," became an immediate viral sensation. It was the fastest branded video to reach 30 million views in the history of the internet, and it went on to accrue well over 100 million views. The video ended up being the most-shared celebrity ad in the world that year, surpassing global brands like Apple, Samsung, and Pepsi — all for a brand that nobody had ever even heard of the night before the video was launched.

And, in the process, we brought the concept of shareability to worldwide attention with one of the biggest stars in the world.

Shareability is how and why content is shared online. It is a concept at the heart of creating meaningful success on the internet and one that I believe in so strongly, I named my company after it. This book will teach you how to embrace the power of shareability and use it to drive massive results. But to truly understand it, we must first look at how we got here and face the reality of the world that we live in.

The One-Way Conversation

Thirty years ago, long before the internet, we lived in a much different world. Television was the dominant medium, and things that we take for granted today, like creating and sharing content on our phones, seemed like a concept straight out of a science fiction novel. In 1989, if you wanted to spread a message or market a product to a national or international audience, you basically had one option — hire an expensive production company to create an even more expensive commercial, and then spend millions of dollars in television or radio ads to push that message out to an audience defined only by which television channel they happened to be tuned in to.

What if you didn't have millions of dollars? Well, you were basically out of luck. All of the media "pipes" of the day, from television and radio to print and billboards, were controlled by major media corporations, and they demanded big dollars for anyone to access them. Even the equipment to produce television-quality content was far beyond the means of all but the biggest brands and the wealthiest individuals.

This reality created a monopolistic marketplace for established brands that had the means to spend money on traditional advertising. In the 1980s and 90s, major brands were easily spending hundreds of millions a year, and *Fortune* 500 companies were collectively spending tens of billions on traditional advertising, almost all of which was going into television. In 2000, for example, General Mills spent 94 percent of its advertising dollars on television, Coca-Cola spent 87 percent, and Anheuser-Busch 86 percent.

This system served to ward off innovation and brand competition, as the high cost of entry made it extremely difficult for new brands or ideas to break into the market. Simply put, there was no way for the little brand, let alone an individual, to be heard on a wide scale.

Then new technology and the internet came along, and they changed everything. Ad blockers like TiVo began disrupting television advertising. A slow, steady decline in TV ratings occurred as people's attention drifted online.

In effect, the internet was the great equalizer. For the first time in human history, everyday people had the same access to the powerful "pipe" to spread their messaging to a national and even international audience.

And then technology put a smartphone in the hands of millions of people. There was an explosion of mobile viewing. Millennials, in particular, were watching most content on their phones and flocking toward 3-minute videos instead of 30-minute television shows. The smartphone was basically a portable movie studio, capable of not only making professional-grade content but pushing it out to the new "pipes" of the internet, the burgeoning social platforms.

For the old guard of advertising, this was chaos.

Major brands found themselves dazed and confused by these rapid changes and ill-equipped to navigate this new world, from Facebook to YouTube to niche players like Hulu, Snapchat, and

Thrillist. Without the full force of the trusted bullhorn of television advertising, the brand identities of *Fortune* 500 companies began to decline. Much of this was because they didn't know how to connect with their consumers. For decades, they had been dumping billions of dollars into a one-way conversation, but they never touched the audience in the way that it now demanded.

And where there is chaos, there is opportunity.

For marketers, this was the biggest opportunity since the advent of television — engaging with people directly via the internet. The internet democratized content, opening up avenues for anyone to reach everyone.

For a while, the new world order was really sweet. In the early days of internet content, there wasn't much competition. When YouTube launched in 2005, the platform's biggest problem was that there wasn't anything to put on it. iPhones wouldn't be invented for another two years. Facebook was still available only to college students, and the idea that brands (let alone regular people) would create and post their own content was still completely foreign. For that reason, most content available online at the time was either mundane or poorly produced. Consequently, when a brand or individual did create something that was unique, it would be widely shared and would garner a lot of attention.

People would watch a video and share it with their friends, causing engagement to spike. This would in turn alert the YouTube algorithm to feature the content further, thereby increasing the viewership and engagement. Once millions of people had watched the content, blogs and the digital press would jump on the bandwagon and "report" on the video as the latest trend or cool thing on the web, sending it even farther up the charts.

It was a beautiful and simple cycle. The most unique videos would get shared across the web with such speed and force that a new term was created to describe what was happening — "going viral" was born.

Going Viral

There was a time when "viral" simply referred to, well, viruses. These tiny parasitic microbes would develop a superior ability not only to infect their hosts but, more important, to spread to new hosts. The idea that a creature so small could spread so quickly to so many people was very powerful, and when small videos started spreading like wildfire, the term was simply adopted, and it stuck. In the modern zeitgeist, this concept is so entrenched that when people hear "viral," they often think of videos first and infectious diseases second.

From around 2008 until 2015, as the internet gained users by the hundreds of millions, viral videos were all the rage. They sprung up from people emailing or texting their friends: "Wow! This is so cool! You gotta watch it!" The first person would then send it to the next person and so forth until it spread so quickly that it reached the point where if you hadn't seen that kooky video of the dog jumping back and forth through a flaming Hula-Hoop, you just had to go online to check it out.

The success of early YouTubers altered the branding landscape. As millennials raised on smartphones turned away from television to more original and outrageous content on the internet, a new generation of self-made media stars was born. This period was fueled by a sense of discovery — young people felt like they were uncovering new talent, rather than having it forced on them by out-of-touch media companies, and this created an audience that was far more vested in the talent's success.

As these YouTubers showed what was possible, brands jumped in and tried to do the same thing, that is, create viral content and build communities of followers. The focus on promoting brands on the internet was all about going viral, getting as many eyeballs on your content as possible. Millions of dollars were spent trying to make ads go viral.

When the very first YouTube video was uploaded, on April 23, 2005, not many people had video cameras, let alone the then-revolutionary delivery system of "broadband" access. But by 2018, more than 1.3 billion people were using YouTube, watching 5 billion videos a day and uploading new content at the astonishing rate of 300 hours of video every minute.

With so much content available at everyone's fingertips, the world became a very noisy place. People became bombarded by content, exposed to as many as 5,000 online ads per day.

For brands this created a tricky issue. Not only are the vast majority of people jaded and immune to traditional commercials, but they are also very sophisticated and adept at filtering the noise. On platforms like Facebook, they swipe up like a serial dater blowing through Tinder, based on a split-second gut call. On YouTube, the only reason they stay is to wait for the skip button to appear in 3 . . . 2 . . . 1, and then it's a quick look and click. Add that to the algorithm changes on the major social networks, which limit the number of people who see your post, and you begin to see the difficult challenge of getting people's attention.

The irony is that while everyone is trying to be noticed, no one gets noticed. In a world with no attention span, even virality has become less valuable.

Remember the woman who bought the Chewbacca mask at Kohl's, put it on while she was in her car, and made a video laughing at herself? At the time, back in 2016, it was the biggest live-stream-

ing video on Facebook ever. It was viewed by 162 million people, more than double the number who saw the second-place video that year. *

She became a major internet sensation, appeared on *The Late Late Show,* and received thousands of dollars in perks from various companies looking to ride the tail of her notoriety. But the shelf life of her fame was about two weeks. She then returned to her normal, everyday life, and now people would be hard-pressed to remember her name. Sometimes viral gets you nowhere.

So how does a brand embrace the dynamics of the internet world and break through all of this noise?

The answer is simple: *Be shareable.*

Being shareable means that you create content with such high value for the people viewing it that they are *compelled* to share it

---

* "Chewbacca Mom" from Candace Payne via Facebook live stream, May 19, 2016.

with their friends. This mindset puts the viewer first and builds a relationship *before* attempting to sell, essentially the opposite of traditional advertising's approach. As you'll learn in this book, understanding shareability and attracting shares are some of the most valuable things you can do for your brand.

Don't take my word for it. Ask the Ayzenberg Group, the firm that delivers the Ayzenberg Earned Media Value Index Report. In an attempt to quantify the value that social media response provided to brands, the report assigns a dollar value to the various actions, such as a Like, a share, or a comment, that people can take on all the different social platforms. For example, in 2018 they gave a VPS (value per share) of $2.58 on tumblr, $2.14 on Facebook, $1.67 on Twitter, $0.91 on YouTube, and $0.10 on Pinterest.

The share is the most coveted action. It commands the highest premium and delivers the most value. That's because a share is what turns your audience into your brand ambassador, engaging them to tacitly recommend your brand messaging to their friends. This "word of mouth" endorsement has always been the gold standard of advertising, because it is the most meaningful.

Being shareable is all about making people lean in rather than click off or swipe past.

All social platforms are built on the concept of sharing. They all promote content that shares well — and people on those platforms will share your brand message if it's crafted right.

That's an incredibly dynamic concept. People will share your brand message. It's the ultimate word-of-mouth marketing — you get the people to do the marketing for you. You give them something of value, something that just so happens to be carrying your brand message, and they share it with their friends, saying, "Hey, check out this cool thing I found!"

You are the cool thing. *You.*

Think about that. You are no longer the ad they all swipe past instantly. Instead, you are the beautiful pebble they find on the beach, the cool new trend they love, the most happening of all the new things.

This evolution past virality is called shareability. Virality is still a good thing, but it is increasingly harder to attain and even more uncontrollable when captured. Shareability, on the other hand, grants predictability and value and allows your message to grow exponentially.

Though virality hasn't totally lost all its magic and can be useful, it's just no longer the top goal for content. Virality will always be a useful mechanism in branding, but chasing virality is a thing of the past. The focus now is on being shareable. That will expand your message, give you a competitive advantage, and grow your brand.

What Do People Share?

Now that you understand the importance of being shareable, the next step is to look at the *types of content* that have been widely shared on the internet. This is not a literal exercise, as certain types of content may have little relevance to your brand or may prove unrealistic for you to execute. But what has succeeded in the past can teach you valuable lessons about how the internet works, and may give you inspiration as to what will work in the future.

In the glory days of online virality, there were essentially five types of content that went to the top of the YouTube charts day after day.

First were Music Videos.

From the early days of YouTube, music videos have dominated the platform and driven hundreds of billions of views. Prior to the internet, artists and labels had been making these short films around hit songs for decades dating back to the MTV era, so they already were skilled at telling their musical stories in 3–4 minute videos, the ideal length for the YouTube platform. When you also consider that the record labels provided substantial budgets to make these videos and celebrity music artists delivered the star power to promote them, it makes perfect sense that music videos and the internet would prove a powerful marriage.

It was a music video, in fact, that was the first YouTube video to surpass 1 billion views, when the South Korean rapper Psy's "Gangnam Style" took the internet by storm in 2012 and was recognized by the Guinness World Records as the video with the most Likes on YouTube that year. *

Want a case study in being shareable? Study "Gangnam Style." In an era when everyone was taking themselves and their music very seriously, Psy, whose real name is Park Jae-sang, did the exact opposite, making fun of not only himself but basically every pop cliché

---

* "Gangnam Style" published on YouTube July 15, 2012, from YG Entertainment Inc.

that has ever existed. And he did this while delivering a catchy tune and a series of ridiculous dance moves that were easy to learn and hilarious to watch. It's no wonder that the song and Psy became an international sensation, topping the music charts in 30 countries and cited by President Obama during a meeting with the South Korean president at the White House as a powerful emblem of Korean culture. Heck, Obama even attempted the dance moves.

The second category was what we affectionately call Adorable Babies. This doesn't literally mean that the videos have to be about babies, but rather about people — often babies — doing or saying cute, funny, or memorable things.

Think of it like a YouTube version of *America's Funniest Home Videos,* where an intimate yet surprising moment is shared with the world. A perfect example of this is one of the most viewed non-music videos on YouTube, titled "Charlie bit my finger — again!" In the video, a young boy named Harry is sitting in a chair with his baby brother, Charlie, on his lap. In the beginning of the video, Harry laughs as Charlie lightly nips at his finger. But as the video continues, Charlie chomps down, sending Harry into screams and tears and then delivering the memorable line to his infant brother — "Charlie! That really hurt!" — to which Charlie responds with a devious laugh. When Harry comes around to a smile at the end the video, it becomes a sweet and familiar portrait of two brothers that any parent could relate to. The video quickly went viral and has driven over 880 million views and has spawned numerous remixes and parodies.

The third category we call Shock and Awe. These are videos that showcase awesome, crazy actions that we haven't seen before.

In the early days of YouTube, this category involved a lot of videos from extreme sports. Clearly, sports has always been a huge part of the viewing ethos, both in America and around the world. The primary traditional sports, including soccer, baseball, American football, basketball, hockey, auto racing, and golf, have been staples of television programming for decades. They have consistently driven some of the highest ratings on television. The Super Bowl attracts 90 million viewers in the United States, and the World Cup and the Olympic Games far more globally.

But in the mid-2000s, emerging sports like skateboarding, BMX, and snowboarding became wildly popular with a young audience, but were not receiving traditional television exposure. The energy drink Red Bull stepped in to fill this void. They championed extreme sports and started to build shareable videos around young athletes doing radical things like a flip on a bike, a jump off a cliff, or a dive out of an airplane. This strategy has been incredibly powerful, driving billions of views and pushing Red Bull to become one of the most successfully branded beverages in the world. With each success, Red Bull grew even bolder with the content that they produced. This led to the epic 2012 stunt titled "Felix Baumgartner's supersonic freefall from 128k." * The video featured daredevil Baumgartner jumping to earth from a helium balloon in the stratosphere. I can't imagine a more shareable headline than that!

* "Felix Baumgartner's supersonic freefall from 128k," published on YouTube October 14, 2012, from Red Bull.

Number four was Prank Videos.

This category was tremendously successful in the early days of YouTube, and still carries on today. We all know that people love surprises, and the early YouTubers discovered that capturing people's reactions to unexpected events was pure internet gold. In the beginning, the pranks were fairly simplistic, like the video "BEST scare prank EVER!!!" Uploaded in 2006, it featured a guy named Andy, who puts on a creepy mask and a hoodie and scares the daylights out of his buddy the precise moment he wakes up.

As this category evolved, the bar was raised and pranksters pushed the limits to break through a growing sea of competition. In 2011, late-night host Jimmy Kimmel engineered a prank in which, on the day after Halloween, parents told their unsuspecting children that they had eaten all of their Halloween candy. The kids' reactions were priceless and the video soared to 60 million views. *

---

* "YouTube Challenge — I Told My Kids I Ate All Their Halloween Candy," published on YouTube November 2, 2011, from *Jimmy Kimmel Live*.

Over the past ten years, prank videos have generated billions of views and turned ordinary people like Jack Vale and Roman Atwood into multimillionaire YouTubers.

Last, but certainly not least, was Comedy Videos.

Comedy, still going strong, has been one of the most successful genres online, and it makes up a sizable percentage of shareable content. This is a broad category, encompassing everything from standup comedians' bits to late-night hosts' monologues to amateur slapstick. Many of the early innovators of new comedic formats on the internet came from the social platform Vine.

One of the biggest acts to come out of Vine was a guy named King Bach. Born in Toronto to Jamaican parents, Bach eventually made his way to Los Angeles, where he joined the Groundlings. His videos were edgy, slapstick comedy built around real-world topics that he took to hyperbolic, illogical conclusions. Videos on Vine were limited to 6 seconds, so Bach's videos were filmed in an ADD style perfect for the YouTube generation. He became so proficient at the format that he accrued over 15 million followers and became the number-one star in the world on Vine. This success then crossed over to YouTube and Instagram, and Bach eventually became a traditional media star as well, appearing on television shows like *House of Lies* and in movies like the spoof comedy hit *Fifty Shades of Black*. He is currently the second-most-followed African American entertainer on social media, right behind Kevin Hart.

Late-night hosts like Jimmy Fallon and Jimmy Kimmel have also found success with short-form comedy on the internet. Armed with television budgets and a Rolodex of celebrity guests, Fallon and Kimmel have created some of the most shareable videos over the past ten years. Kimmel created the memorable self-deprecating format "Celebrities Read Mean Tweets," where celebrities appear on camera and read real, unflattering tweets about themselves. Fallon also created "Lip Sync Battles," where celebrities basically try to outperform each other by dancing while lip-syncing a well-known song. The videos have been so successful that they launched a television show spinoff on Spike TV.

Although these categories have been widely successful for many people, bear in mind they may not be the right fit for you. Most brands, for instance, wouldn't be comfortable pranking their customers or launching a man from the stratosphere. Even comedy can be a tough dynamic to pull off for many companies.

And don't forget: The early days of the internet featured a lot of content that was, to put it politely, sophomoric. Many of the most viewed and shared videos up until 2010 showed people jumping out of planes or getting kicked in the groin. The second wave of internet content is more productive, giving people the chance to learn, be inspired, and find the better attributes of humanity. The themes of this content are more widely used to promote brands.

Shareable Brandable Content

Fortunately, the internet has matured and expanded, and several popular new styles of shareable content are far more brand-friendly. Chief among them are Inspirational Videos, Educational Videos, and what we call Good Samaritan Videos.

One of the early pioneers of inspirational content was the TED Conference, which features TED Talks, speeches addressing the topics of technology, entertainment, and design (hence the term TED). These talks have attracted some of the biggest names in these fields, including Elon Musk, Bill Gates, and Stephen Hawking. Along with inspiration, the talks often deliver practical information and guiding principles applicable to even the most common human dilemmas.

An example of an immensely shareable TED Talk was Simon

Sinek's 2009 talk titled "How Great Leaders Inspire Action." The video is simply just Sinek, a relatively unknown author at the time, on stage at a TED event in Puget Sound, Washington, equipped with only a blank sheet of paper and a black marker. Sinek poses a very simple question to the audience: why are some people and organizations more innovative, more influential, and more profitable than others? He then goes on to illustrate what he calls the "Golden Circle," explaining how successful leaders like Steve Jobs and Martin Luther King Jr. realized that people won't truly buy in to a product, movement, or idea until they understand the WHY behind it. Sinek's production quality was extremely low rent, just a marker scribbling circles on a large pad of paper on an easel, but the wisdom was pure gold, catapulting the video to over 40 million views and launching his publishing career into the stratosphere.

Educational content is a broad, fairly self-explanatory category that involves videos created with the intent of teaching the audience about a particular subject or making them smarter about a topic. While this may sound boring, some very smart people have used this method to present valuable information in an entertaining and shareable fashion.

The YouTube channel Vsauce, created by an educator named Michael Stevens from Kansas, illustrates this point nicely. Stevens has figured out how to investigate out-of-the-ordinary questions about math, psychology, and philosophy in fun, thought-provoking ways. Most of his videos are titled with a question, such as "What Is the Speed of Dark?" or "What Can You Do Without a Brain?" They use science and creative thinking to examine the way we look at the world. Stevens's offbeat persona has resonated with a global audience, and in 2018 the Vsauce channel reached 13 million subscribers.

Another YouTube channel doing education differently is Smarter Every Day. Launched in 2007 by an American engineer named Destin Sandlin, the channel explores the everyday world through the eyes of science. Sandlin has tackled topics ranging from how tattooing works to why cats flip in the air to the truth about toilet swirl. And he does it all with a contagious style that has racked up over 400 million views.

At Shareability, we went a step further in 2016 when we partnered with Prince Ea to take on the establishment of public education. Prince Ea, whose real name is Richard Williams, is a spoken-word artist who makes message-driven videos and has a significant following on Facebook. The project was funded by Neste, a Finnish energy company whose philanthropic mission is to reform education.

The headline was bold — "We wanted to put the failing education system in the U.S. on trial." Richard wrote a rap poem titled "I Just Sued the School System!!!" and we shot a video with him as a prosecutor in a courtroom, where he presents his case against American education. "Ladies and gentlemen of the jury, today on trial we have modern day schooling," he opens.

The unique message, combining bold language and stunning visuals, made quite the impact. The video, titled "The People vs. the School System," was ripped and reposted across the internet, ultimately hitting 350 million views and 9 million shares, making it one of the most shared PSAs (public service announcements) in the history of the internet. The video proved that even the most seemingly boring topics can ignite widespread sharing if presented in an entertaining way. The results also show that new avenues are opening for videos sponsored by corporations, foundations, and activists to create and share content on social issues that might otherwise be ignored.

When done right, educational content can be dynamic and shareable, which is why it has been one of the fastest-growing genres on the internet.

The Good Samaritan category encompasses feel-good videos

that showcase an individual or group going out of their way to help someone else and make that person's life better. This type of content has been gaining steam over the past few years, possibly in response to the polarizing political content of recent election cycles.

(A quick note about political content. We're not going to analyze the virality of political content in this book, as a large portion of it traffics in negativity, fear, and division, which are not useful to expanding a brand.)

An early example of Good Samaritan content is the 2006 video by PeaceOnEarth123 called "Free Hugs Campaign." In it, a bearded young man, wearing glasses and a sports coat, goes to a public square holding a sign that says "Free Hugs." The video shows him walking awkwardly through the crowd, who either ignore him or give him a laugh as they head in the other direction. That all changes when an elderly lady stops and gives him a kind word and a hug. Before long, the floodgates break open and everyone is hugging, with some wild and joyous variations. The video, set to a song by the Sick Puppies, has gone on to more than 70 million views and proved that a small act of kindness can indeed spark a large-scale response.

At Shareability, we love Good Samaritan content and have had great success building feel-good videos with brands like Hyundai, AT&T, and Adobe. One of my favorites is the campaign we created for Adobe Photoshop, focused on lending a helping hand to people who were victimized when Hurricane Harvey decimated parts of Houston. The Facebook video, titled "Hurricane Harvey Restoration Project," shows high school students setting out to restore photographs for families affected by the hurricane. Using Adobe Photoshop, the students repair and restore treasured photos that had been soaked and ruined as flooding overtook many houses in the community. The students then present new framed photographs to their surprised owners as tears and appreciation flow on both sides. The video soared to over 7 million views, led to great national media coverage, and offered a poignant reminder that in times of tragedy, that it's the little things that can make a big difference.

In short, there are many ways to be shareable. Trends are always changing, but by studying what has worked in the past and what others are doing successfully, you can evolve your own strategy and be best positioned to make successful content that an audience will not only watch but will want to share.

Understanding and using the principles of shareability are the most important tools that you can master to have success on the internet. Getting people to share your content is critical to expanding your reach and finding an audience that is invested in you. We like to say sharing is the holy grail, because when people share, they care . . . and when they care, they buy. This mindset involves faith because you need to trust that your returns may come later. Instead of coming out and hitting someone over the head with your message, you engage people first and then build a relationship with them. In this way, shareability is essentially the opposite of advertising—call it the anti-advertising. Advertising is a one-way street from a brand to a customer, while sharing is a multi-lane highway, in which a friend recommends a brand to others and thereby expands the reach of that brand by bringing it to new customers.

If you read this book and take away only one thing, I hope it is this: *Be shareable.*

Rule 2

Understand the Science

Now that you understand the importance of shareabililty and have seen examples of shareable content, let's ask a deeper question: Why do people share?

Understanding this is essential to making your content spread organically, but the reason people share may surprise you. In our experience people generally share for one reason: They are being selfish.

But wait, isn't sharing the total opposite of being selfish?

Sure, the act of sharing is selfless. Sharing is caring, after all. But the *reason* you are doing it is 100 percent selfish.

Take a generous act of sharing, like cutting a sandwich in two and giving half to a person in need. Very selfless act, right? Especially since you were hungry and you actually worked to earn the money that bought the sandwich. You have just done something wonderful. How did that make you feel?

I bet it made you feel good.

Do you think you gave away your sandwich because it made other people feel good or because the *act* of giving it made you feel good about yourself? If you're truly honest, it's probably the latter.

Studies have shown that, for the giver, it is better to give than to receive. In 2017, University of Zurich reseachers put this theory to the test. They clinically surveyed the current mood of 50 men and women and also had them undergo MRIs. They then gave all of them money, with a condition attached. Half were told to spend it all on themselves, and the other half were told to spend it on someone else. At the end of the process, the group was tested again. The givers' moods were uniformly better, and their MRIs uniformly showed greater activity in the portion of the brain associated with altruism.

So if most sharing is, at its heart, selfish, how is sharing still connected to caring? Actually, it is and it's connected in an even stronger way — and one that is especially beneficial to brands. You share something because you care — not about the person you are sharing with, but *about the thing you are sharing*. For instance, if you share the latest Jay-Z/Beyoncé collaboration, you aren't doing this because you care about your friends being in tune with the latest hip music video. Rather, you are doing it because you are a fan.

This is an important concept and one that plays right into the hands of the strategies of Shareability. By making people care about our company's campaigns, they then share them, and when they share, they are telling the world that it is something worthy of everyone's time and attention. In other words, your brand is worthy of people's time and attention. That is the biggest endorsement anyone can give.

Building "Digital Walls"

To understand how these social dynamics play out in sharing online content, we need to understand how the "bedroom wall" has evolved into the "digital wall."

In the 1980s and 90s, the walls of a teenager's room told you exactly who they were and, even more so, who they wanted to be. For boys, there might have been posters of Kurt Cobain, Michael Jordan, and the Terminator. A girl might have taped up pictures of Britney Spears, Leonardo DiCaprio, and a rotating set of torn-out magazine pages featuring the boy bands of the moment. For each new band that broke, or screen hottie that dazzled, or fashion trend that hit, they would alter their décor.

That culture has vanished. Now the bedroom walls of everyone, from teens to millennials to baby boomers, are their social media profiles, that is, their "digital walls." These digital walls define how we present ourselves, from the descriptions of who we are, to the photos, content, and links that we post. Every liked or shared video says something about the person who likes or shares it, meaning that we post and share not just the stuff that we love, but more important, the stuff we want people to know that we love. It is how we represent who we are to the world, and ultimately how we want people to view us.

The critical point to understand is that people like and share internet content not for others, but rather to define themselves, and for how it makes them look and feel. In short, they do it for self-serving or selfish reasons.

Understanding this human dynamic of how sharing makes us social and how it presents us to the world is essential to creating shareable content. We need to put ourselves in the shoes of our potential audience and to consider what value they would get out of sharing a piece of our content.

Let's say a brand creates a traditional commercial that promotes the benefits of a new skin-care line. The video is shot beautifully, using the latest cameras and lighting techniques, and tells people how amazing this product is. Will people share that commercial?

Well, clearly sharing that video would be good for the company, but what benefit does a teenage girl from Milwaukee obtain from sharing it? Why would she ever do that? The obvious answer is that she probably wouldn't, but I hesitate to say "obvious" because most brands still clearly don't understand the dynamics of sharing.

Not to pick on anyone in particular, but let's take J.Crew. Who doesn't love a brand that makes reasonably priced clothes you can actually wear and that last? In recent years, with its Ludlow suit and better-cut women's clothes, J.Crew has become a staple of many younger working persons' wardrobes. So the brand has some credibility to make shareable content that resonates with millennials.

Yet, last year, J.Crew posted a video on Facebook featuring its Slim Perfect T-shirt that played, in my opinion, like a boring ad. The video featured a guy talking about how well the T-shirt fit and what kind of cotton was used. The result? The video had exactly 1 share out of its 1.8 million followers. Oh, it also had 1 comment, which simply said: "Rubbish." That comment pretty much sums it up!

Now contrast that with the video for a campaign that we executed for a pet food company called Freshpet a few years back, titled "Freshpet Holiday Feast." Freshpet is a New Jersey–based firm that makes fresh, all-natural pet food, so fresh in fact that it needs to be refrigerated. This in itself was a very shareable product concept. In fact, Freshpet was one of the first companies to put refrigerators into the pet food aisle at various retail stores like Target and Walmart.

Like J.Crew, Freshpet has a solid product, one that had gotten high reviews and had built a loyal following of users. However, Freshpet's challenge was that very few consumers knew about their product. To alleviate this problem, they had tried traditional advertising, which did give them some lift, but they didn't have the budget to break through to a mass audience.

When they hired us, we asked ourselves, "What would dog lovers love to see on the internet?" Notice that the original question was not "What is great about Freshpet products that people on the internet would like to see?" That type of question comes later. What our research told us is that dog lovers would enjoy watching pets act like humans. From that one insight, "Freshpet Holiday Feast" was born.

We created a video where pets acting like humans, with human hands and clothes, were gathered around a table for a holiday meal. The video featured 13 dogs and a cat, with each playing an archetype of a friend or relative who would be present at a holiday party. The animals were all dressed in holiday attire. This hilarious cast included the drunken uncle, the distracted teenager using a cellphone, the love-struck couple, and of course, the "cat boss" at the head of the table.

The video was basically a silent movie set to festive holiday music that showcased the interactions of all the guests sitting down to a feast of Freshpet food. The video was around 2 minutes long and very lightly branded, and it finished with an end card sending viewers to the Freshpet website. As an additional twist, we partnered with the local Humane Society to supply the dogs and the cat, and all of the pets featured in the video were available for adoption (and, in fact, were adopted).

So instead of focusing on Freshpet, we focused on what pet owners wanted and gave them an entertaining holiday video with a feel-good twist. Does this sound like something that pet owners would share? Well, they shared it like crazy. The video has become one of the most successful branded holiday videos of all time. It has skyrocketed to over 100 million views and millions of shares, while receiving positive coverage around the world in media outlets from ABC to Mashable to the *Huffington Post*.

People shared the Freshpet video because it was funny, and it made them laugh. By extension, they were showing that they had a sense of humor while also bolstering their digital wall.

That's all great, you say, but what about Freshpet? What did they get out of it?

More than they ever imagined. Store locator traffic for Freshpet product increased over 3,000 percent. When the company later went public, the CEO talked to Bloomberg about Shareability and the success of the video. Every year since, the video gets re-uploaded at Christmas and goes viral all over again, racking up tens of millions of additional views and awareness for Freshpet.

In sum, the video had a real and measurable impact on the bottom line. That's the power of shareability in action.

The Five Shareable Emotions

Marketers have long used emotion to engage consumers and encourage them to connect with brands. At my company, we spend an unhealthy amount of time thinking about why people share content. We are constantly reading, researching, and testing the latest trends and science to better understand how to gain an unfair advantage in getting people to share.

Numerous people have written at length about the emotions that drive sharing. Through all of our work and by studying the various reports on shareable feelings, we have discovered that there are five keys that drive a disproportionate number of shares online. We call them the Five Shareable Emotions, and they are a never-ending focus for us as we work with major brands and celebrities.

Understanding these emotions and what triggers them can make all the difference in how your content is received and shared online.

1. Happiness

The first shareable emotion is happiness. Happiness content is exactly what you think it would be — it's content that makes people happy. When you're happy, what do you want to do? Very often, you want to share that feeling with a friend! People love to share things that will bring joy to people they care about, because that in turn will make them feel good about themselves.

Videos that bring happiness are no different. Especially today, when the polarized content found in both social and traditional media has created the impression that the world is littered with constant negativity and division. (It's not — the world is statistically a much happier and more unified place than ever before, but that's a subject for another time.) In this perceived harsh climate, happiness content is incredibly powerful. When you can put a smile on someone's face or bring even a small moment of positivity into their day, it can have a big impact. And we're eager to make our loved ones and friends feel happy.

This category includes all of the Adorable Babies content that we talked about earlier, along with what we like to call Internet Candy — fun, often silly or charming content that doesn't make you think too hard, like "Freshpet Holiday Feast."

Another example of how we put this into practice is our work for the Olympic Games.

The Olympic Games is one of the most recognized and respected brands in the world, and every two years the games take center stage on a global basis, recognizing athletic achievement. For that 16-day period of competition, the games are literally the biggest show on earth. The challenge is the time in between Olympic Games, when the torch burns far less bright. The International Olympic Committee's content arm turned to us as they launched the Olympic Channel, a digital network meant to keep viewers and fans engaged between games. We knew that the type of athletic content that was so talked about during the games wouldn't play nearly as well in the "off-season," so we designed a video campaign that tapped into the pure emotion of joy on a universal level.

Our brain trust came up with the idea of babies competing in Olympic events, and the ensuing video delivered one of the highest Shareability scores we have ever had. We tapped into the joy of cute babies set against the thrilling environment of Olympic events to create a piece of content unlike any other, which elicited smiles and caused shares. "Baby Olympics" became one of the biggest viral successes of 2017, garnering over 150 million views and 3 million shares worldwide.

For brands, using happiness content is almost the exact opposite of advertising. Typically in traditional advertising, the brand is beating its own chest and telling the targeted audience why they should buy their product. This leads to a very one-sided conversation with minimal value to viewers. More often than not, they turn the other way and run.

By producing a feel-good video instead of a commercial, the brand is saying, "I'm making this for you, the audience, so that I can hopefully brighten up your day." This transforms the content of a selfish commercial into a selfless act of kindness, and what happens when you do something nice for someone? They want to pay you back. We've seen again and again that when brands invest against their audience and give them something of value, something that is selfless, the audience will pay them back tenfold.

They may repay you with their attention, their actions, or their wallet, but any way you slice it, you will have taken the first step toward building a real relationship with your customers.

One important element of this — and one that brands understand and can quantify — is called brand sentiment. This is a measure of what the general population, or a specific demographic, thinks of your brand. How they *feel* about it. It's well established that when consumers feel positive about a brand, they are far more likely to spend their money on that brand rather than on the competition. Creating this type of happiness content can accomplish exactly that. It makes the brand more likable, more relatable, more . . . *human*.

We have seen the impact of this time and time again. When brand sentiment goes up, sales go up. These two metrics are connected in a very direct and measurable way.

To create happiness content, start with the audience you want to reach, and figure out what type of content they enjoy on the internet. Then give them that. Of course, you also need to figure out how to connect the brand or product to the content in a meaningful way, but you'd be surprised how seamless that often tends to be.

2. Awe

Awe is the second shareable emotion. It is an emotion of reverence or respect, often coupled with a hint of fear and wonder. It can be triggered by novel, crazy, or interesting things that people have never seen before. They are often unique acts performed by animals or humans, impressive or selfless acts that make you say "Wow!" In short, things that are, well . . . awesome.

I'll never forget the first time I saw and heard the 2012 video for the Red Bull Stratos Project:

> "Medical systems green." Pause. "There's the release."
>
> Cautious applause scatters across the control room as a helium balloon is launched into space, carrying daredevil Felix Baumgartner.
>
> "Successful rise . . . Felix current altitude 25,300 feet and climbing."
>
> "We are at 108,000 feet . . . there's an issue with heat in the face plate . . . mission continuing . . . the decision has been made. Felix will jump."
>
> Felix opened the capsule door. On the large screen in the control room came his POV: Earth.
>
> " . . . jumper away . . ."
>
> Out he went into the stratosphere.
>
> " . . . speed 650 mph . . . speed 725 . . . speed 729 . . . Felix at a stable descent . . ."

Then came what seemed like an eternity.

"Chute deployed . . . Felix is back to earth safely."

Applause rang out as everyone in the control room watched the image of Felix safely back on the ground. Felix maneuvered himself to his knees and then bowed.

While Chuck Yeager was the first man to reach supersonic speed in an aircraft, Felix Baumgartner had just become the first man to reach supersonic speed — without an airplane. Falling to earth in nothing but a spacesuit, he hit a speed of 1,357 kilometers per hour (843.6 mph, or Mach 1.25) and broke the world free-fall record.

This type of awe was the stock-in-trade of early YouTube videos. In the first days of Shareability, we worked with a young filmmaker turned YouTuber by the name of devinsupertramp. He was the king of "Wow!" His videos would feature young people doing adventurous things that didn't seem possible (or wise) and having a blast doing it. One of his earliest hits showed Devin and his friends (including Shareability cofounder Cameron Manwaring) building a giant rope swing under a massive rock arch in Utah. In beautiful cinematic style, the video showed Devin's team attaching the rope and then proceeding to launch off the side of a cliff, naturally with views from the GoPro cameras on their bodies, for promotional impact. You can check it out at https://youtu.be/4B36Lr0Unp4. It has been ten years since the video launched, and it still elicits a "Wow!"

Using this type of awe can be very powerful, but the truth is, it's no longer a guarantee for success. In the early days of online video, any time you made a video that made people say "Wow!" your share rate would go through the roof and you'd have a hit on your hands. With each passing year, as more and more content floods the internet and the competition for eyeballs gets more and more intense, it becomes more and more difficult to pull it off.

When devinsupertramp started jumping off cliffs with his friends in 2011, he was the only guy doing it (or at least doing it well). Today, there are hundreds of thousands of channels on all kinds of social media platforms, all fighting to break through and deliver the biggest and most impressive awe video of the week. There are large media companies specializing in scraping the internet for every piece of impressive cellphone footage showing people performing daring, crazy, jaw-dropping acts and licensing them in bulk. If you want to compete, just having a bunch of good-looking young people jump off a cliff doesn't cut it anymore. Now, you need to really stand out in order to break through the noise.

So how do you do that? Well, for us, we moved away from the physical "shock and awe" and into the more emotionally impressive. Don't get me wrong, we still blow stuff up or pull off amazing feats of physical engineering from time to time, but as the world has become more and more noisy and everyone is yelling for attention, we have become quieter. We have stopped throwing people out of helicopters and started tapping into a completely different level of "Wow."

This approach, of course, swings to the opposite end of the spectrum. It doesn't rely on being cinematic or physically impressive at all, but rather on showing that People Are Awesome through what they can do for others and the positive impact they can have. How many times have you seen videos where students do something awesome for their teacher? Or videos of people dedicating their lives to rescuing the coral reefs, living with an endangered species, or building musical instruments for underprivileged children? If this sounds like stuff that shows up in your social feeds, congratulations, you are just like other humans and you enjoy watching people doing wonderful, selfless acts to help others.

The insight to lean our client companies in new directions like this, to buck the common trends and to find a new niche to explore, comes from a combination of factors, chiefly our obsessive monitoring of the internet and the smart young people we employ. But you don't need a staff or an office full of clever people in order to do this for yourself.

The insight that drove this new version of awe came from our lead creative, Joel Bergvall, when he was simply looking inside himself to see what moved him. Specifically, he was revisiting the *Lord of the Rings* trilogy with his wife and kids. You may be familiar with the moment at the climax of the third movie, when the entire fellowship stands at the gates of Mordor, with Frodo and Sam on the inside, fighting their way to the mountain to destroy the Ring. They know that they need to draw Sauron's eye away from his own lands, but they are outnumbered and any action is a complete suicide mission. Aragorn turns to the rest of the crew and says, "For Frodo." With that, they rush their unbeatable enemy with all their might, the tiny hobbits leading the pack, racing into certain death to give their friend even the smallest and most fleeting of chances.

It's arguably the emotional peak of the entire series, and in watching it unfold, and recognizing his emotional response to it, Joel realized that "people doing selfless things for others" was the core element at play. We have since taken this individual insight, coupled it with our social intelligence, and boiled it down to a category that fits squarely into the emotion of awe, which we can now tap into in order to create highly shareable videos.

One example of how we have implemented this is the video we did for Adobe that I mentioned in Chapter 1. Adobe came to us and said, "We want to promote our Photoshop software to students." We took this very limited brief and looked at the audience they were trying to reach to see what type of content they might like and what emotion we might be able to tap into. It was very clear to us that awe was high on the list and that our People Are Awesome subcategory would be a perfect fit. With that, we landed on the idea of a group of students using the power of Photoshop to restore photographs that had been damaged in the still very recent Hurricane Harvey. We developed a structure where we would get to meet the affected people, see the students work on their photos, and then have the climax be the students bringing back the restored photographs, now printed and framed, to the people who thought the photos were lost forever.

The resulting video was an absolute tearjerker, to the point that when we show it in meetings, we still try not to look at the screen. Even though we have seen it hundreds of times, it still puts a lump in our throats. This emotion translated into a huge success for Adobe, which is now a recurring client of ours.

3. Empathy

The third shareable emotion is empathy. Many people confuse empathy with sympathy, but they are not the same. When you are sympathetic, you feel for someone's situation even though you haven't met them and may not know how they feel. Sympathy can be broad and impersonal, but empathy is specific and deeply personal, making it much more powerful. It's the ability to put yourself in someone else's shoes, to truly understand their feelings about a subject, and to experience those feelings yourself. When you empathize, you are having a feeling similar to the other person's, making an emotional connection, and you can have this without even being sympathetic to their specific plight or opinion.

Empathy can be a tricky emotion to convey genuinely, but when it's done right, empathy is a powerful sharing tool because people want to connect with other people in meaningful ways.

Here's an example. Heineken set out to break down stereotypes and to put empathy to the test in its 2017 "Worlds Apart" campaign. The company embarked on the campaign with the help of Dr. Chris Brauer, director of innovation at Goldsmiths, University of London, who specializes in the study of human behavior. Heineken wanted to find out if people with an entrenched point of view could become more receptive to an opposing point of view by interacting with someone who held that perspective. In other words, could they become more empathetic? Brauer's research showed that if people first found common ground, then they would be more empathetic to someone who held an opposing belief.*

Heineken then shot a 4-minute video that starts out by asking, "Can two strangers with opposing views prove that there's more that unites than divides us?" In the video, they paired six strangers in groups of two. The pairs knew nothing about each other, but viewers were shown clips of them taking staunchly opposing points of view on a topic. A man who calls feminism "man hating" is paired with a feminist. A climate change denier goes so far as to say that people who do believe in climate change should go work on credible problems that actually exist. That individual is, of course, introduced to a climate change activist. A transgender woman meets a man who sees the issue of gender identity in total black and white.

First, each pair is introduced and asked to follow provided instructions on how to build a stool. Next, they build stools together, then are told to sit down on the stools and describe themselves, using five adjectives. As they expand on the adjectives, they get to know each other and begin to open up about personal details, like the sometimes troubling circumstances in which they grew up. In short, they begin to converse and to empathize with a new friend. The pairs are then given another task to complete together, such as building a bar. Bit by bit, their budding friendship begins to grow.

Of course, the kicker comes when they are shown video clips, which viewers have already seen, in which the new friend espouses

---

* Brandingmag.com, "Good Campaign of the Week: Heineken 'Worlds Apart,'" April 23, 2017. https://brandingmag.com/2017/04/23/good-campaign-of-the-week-heineken-worlds-apart/.

a strong opinion that is diametrically and dramatically opposed to their own. As they digest what they have just seen, the pairs are then given a choice: they can either leave . . . or they can discuss their differences over a beer. They all choose to stay and are shown talking and beginning to empathize even more.

This video, done in partnership with a nonprofit organization called The Human Library, which challenges stereotypes through conversations, was a huge hit precisely because it put unbridled empathy on display.

This core of human emotion can be channeled in many ways, but it often boils down to a sense of belonging. A story that creates a desire for belonging in the audience will resonate in a way that invites others to also belong. In the case of the Heineken ad, it's not so much about subscribing to a particular point of view or set of beliefs, but rather about having a sense of human belonging.

By putting our differences on display and showing the human ability to look past the strongest prejudice or difference of opinion, the video tells us that we all belong to the same world, that we all share a human experience, and that it's important to embrace that.

This all goes back to the teenage wall: People share because it represents how they would like to be perceived. They want to show that they too are inclusive, that they can look past differences and have a real dialogue, even with those individuals who have fundamentally different beliefs or values. This is a positive reflection on humankind, and sharing this content reflects positively on the sharer.

4. Curiosity

Curiosity may have killed the cat, but it sure as hell has created a ton of internet candy. It is also responsible for much of human evolution, so there is no way to overstate the importance of this emotion. The *American Heritage Dictionary* defines "curiosity" as "a desire to know or learn." This naturally bleeds into every video we make by the nature of needing to capture people's attention. The job of the first frame of every video is to make people curious about the next frame. The first 3 seconds pull you in for the first 7, which gets you to 15, 30, and so on. Sparking curiosity is a natural part of storytelling because if you cannot do that, no one will want to hear your tale.

Capitalizing on curiosity in video starts with the headline (which we will cover in Rule 5: Crush the Headline). This is what captures people's attention and makes them curious enough to lean in, click play, and take a look.

Next is understanding that much of our social media is "feed based," meaning the video starts playing the moment you scroll to it. This is important: The first few seconds of the video had better spark some instant curiosity in your audience, or they will move on before they even notice you were there.

The same is true for your poster frame. That's the still image that displays if you happen to be connecting from your phone but without Wi-Fi connection, and if your settings are tuned to "not autoplay videos" when you are using cellular data. That may seem like a level of specificity too technical, but it's the kind of vital consideration that can make or break a video. This was always true on YouTube, where the thumbnail was key, and while it's less important for feed-based platforms, it still remains a huge consideration.

So what about curiosity itself makes for good video content? Well, one big answer that may surprise you is education. Remember that curiosity is a strong desire to *know* or to *learn* something. And you thought education was boring!

As an example, let's take a deeper look at a video we did with the spoken-word artist, poet, and filmmaker known as Prince Ea. He was the ambassador for an education program sponsored by the Finnish energy company Neste. Together we created what conventional wisdom dubbed an impossible video. It was a 6-minute PSA that took place in a single location and consisted of one person speaking on the current state of our educational system. Sounds riveting, right?

Well, 350 million views and 9 million shares later, the video titled "The People vs. the School System" is now the most shared PSA of all time, so clearly something was working. What was it? You guessed it: curiosity.

The video starts with a close-up of a goldfish and a quote from Albert Einstein (the attribution may be questionable, but that's not the point). It then reveals the setting: a courtroom where Prince Ea is putting school on trial in front of a gallery of parents and a jury of kids. As Prince Ea speaks, he weaves a masterful tale of learning, and with every new line he delivers an unexpected and interesting point of view that makes you think. From the opening line on, every word he utters makes you lean in, curious as to what he might say next and what the overall conclusion might be. Through the subtle reveal of interesting details, and by gradually introducing all the players and including props and graphics, the piece builds to a powerful crescendo and a standing ovation.

The reason people watch the video is curiosity. They are initially curious about the goldfish, the words, the setting, the people ... then they become even more curious about the points being made and what might come next. The fact that the dialogue is also informative causes you to lean in with more curiosity. Your brain is firing dopamine at you because the video makes you feel *smart*. It educates you, but it does so in a way that makes you feel like you are discovering key information, and that makes the human mind very excited.

You then go on to share the video because not only does it make you look smart, but it will also spark that same feeling of curiosity in others — and that means you are sharing something of real value, which also makes you feel good about yourself.

Not bad for a PSA about the state of education.

5. Surprise

Based on our track record, you could argue that surprise should be our number-one emotion, or at least the most obvious one.

In the digital world, there is nothing more powerful than a human reaction, and no reaction is more powerful than surprise.

It can come in the form of a revelation, a new understanding, from unexpected joy or a simple scare. The best videos combine more than one type of surprise for maximum impact.

Let's take a look at the campaign that Shareability did for Cricket Wireless, "Unexpected John Cena IRL (In Real Life)," as an example. This idea came through our brain trust and was based on the "Unexpected John Cena" meme made popular by the now defunct short-form video-hosting service Vine. The meme consisted of a video clip, followed by John Cena's famous WWE entrance, complete with music.

The initial clip could be anything you could think of, ranging from old movies to cartoons and YouTube clips. These clips all had one thing in common: they all led to some form of introductory phrase or action. This ranged from Batman saying "I'm . . ." to an airline safety ad saying "the panels above you will open, revealing . . ." or simply a toddler fisherman being surprised by his catch clapping him in the face with its fin. These clips were then immediately followed by an abrupt cut to a WWE announcer screaming "John Cena!!," coupled with John's introductory music and visuals.

In other words, surprise was a key element of this meme. It was called "Unexpected John Cena" after all, the joke being that he would always seem to pop up and appear in the most unlikely places, such as at the tail end of any odd video clip you could imagine.

When Cricket came to us and said that we had four hours with John Cena to film the entire campaign, the meme had gone mainstream. We didn't have the faintest idea what the video could be about yet. We did know, however, that if we could tap into that same element of surprise that fueled the meme itself, then we would have something shareable. And if we could somehow stage that surprise with real people in the real world, then we would be sure to have a hit.

Here's how we broke it down:

Surprise number one would be John's acknowledgment that the meme existed, something he hadn't done before.

Surprise number two was that a major celebrity such as John would embrace an internet trend and bring it to life, especially when many perceived the trend itself as making fun of his persona.

Surprise number three would have to come from the video itself and how we would bring the meme to life. Because we were doing "Unexpected John Cena IRL (In Real Life)," we would have to utilize John in some totally unexpected and surprising way.

The fourth and fifth surprises both had to come from the people in the video, the ones who were actually surprised by John. They would add our fourth layer of surprise in a moment of adrenaline-fueled shock, as John jumped out or appeared in some other unexpected way. This would be followed by a fifth layer of surprise — we would make sure to cast huge fans of our star, people who would be starstruck and go nuts seeing him in person.

Now that we knew the shareable emotion and the parameters, we could work backward to create the actual idea. As always, the simplest ideas are the best, and in this we could not have made it more obvious: We would get a bunch of John Cena fans to audition for a fake role as Cricket Ambassadors for the new John Cena Store on Cricket Wireless. They would be asked to read a WWE-style introduction to a poster of John, and at the right moment, John himself would rip through the poster and appear in real life.

Setting the video in a Cricket store meant the brand was naturally integrated, with branding everywhere, something that drove Cricket's appreciation as the video racked up over 220 million views and 4 million engagements.

The video was so successful that even after Cricket's deal with John ended and the official video had been taken down, nearly 7,000 ripped uploads still existed, and the video is still spreading. As of this writing, more than two years after the initial launch, 76 new copies have just been found over the past 30 days.

However, the most important statistic comes directly from the client, Cricket Wireless. They told us that the conversion rates on the actual John Cena Store that came from traffic generated by our video was 300 percent more effective than any other advertising asset they had in the market. That's real, measurable bottom-line impact through the simple power of surprise.

Other Emotions That Enter the Equation

There are obviously many other emotions that trigger someone to share internet content. Joy, gratitude, admiration, hope, and pride are clear contenders. One of the strongest emotions that can trigger sharing is anger. Though the data regularly shows that positive content is more widely shared than negative content, tapping into anger can increase sharing on a large scale in a hurry — but in truth, it's very difficult to make anger work in a positive manner for a brand.

Anger is a high-arousal emotion that makes people take action, both in everyday life and in their online sharing, but most brands don't want to make people angry. In fact, we don't use anger in our campaigns because driving people from anger to a positive action is exceedingly tricky.

Of course, anger *can* be a powerful tool for a cause if you're trying to move people to action and to cause positive change. This is often the case in tragic events, such as the 2018 shooting at Marjory

Stoneman Douglas High School in Parkland, Florida, which claimed the lives of 17 innocent kids and staff. Several videos were posted and heavily shared in the immediate aftermath of the shooting, many taking a stand on gun-related issues. Many people who saw the videos were angry and wanted to do something about it, and as a result the movement to introduce meaningful gun legislation has become bigger and stronger than ever before.

While the videos may have provoked powerful emotions and resulted in millions of shares, this is not a reliable route for brands because anger often results in shares derived from news events that can be polarizing. Brands, of course, want to be inclusive. They would like to sell their wares to people on both sides of any aisle.

Sadness is another common reaction to seeing content online, but sadness on its own is not a shareable emotion. It actually decreases sharing because compared to anger, it is considered a low-arousal emotion. When you watch something sad, you shut down. People are not in a sharing mood when they are sad, as no one wants to share their sadness. However, if you take an inherently sad story and turn that sadness into pride or hope, then it becomes shareable. This is evident in our Adobe video about photo restoration.

These five core shareable emotions — happiness, awe, empathy, curiosity, and surprise — are the primary drivers of positive sharing for brands. Understanding and mastering these emotions will bring results. The next time you share something, test yourself and see if one of these elements is the reason. If nothing else, it will help make you feel less selfish.

Rule 3

Focus on Value

Three strangers walked through the door of a Cricket Wireless store in South Central Los Angeles — and into one of the craziest videos that we had ever dreamed up.

You know the setup of this one already — an open casting call for superfans of WWE superstar John Cena to audition to be Cricket Ambassadors for the John Cena Store on Cricket Wireless. Little did they know that their hero was just a few feet away, on the other side of a paper-thin tear-away wall, listening to every word they said.

I was playing the role of director, calling the fans up one by one and asking them questions about their love for Cena. I would then have them passionately introduce the poster wall behind them (with a life-size image of Cena) as if the legend was actually there.

With each group, I would go through the same process. I would ask them to introduce themselves and then ask questions about what they liked or admired about John Cena. I would build up their energy to the point where they were screaming with excitement as they made their introductions. And then, just as that excitement reached fever pitch, John Cena would burst through the wall and give them the surprise of a lifetime. It was a day that I'll never forget.

In the last chapter, we talked about the surprise elements of this video and particularly the reactions of the people who were surprised in real life. Their reactions were pure internet gold. There is something magical about capturing surprise and unadulterated excitement in raw form. However, if you take a step back and look at the core philosophy of Shareability that made this Cena video into such a massive hit, surprise is only part of the story.

Surprise may have been the key emotion, but much like happiness, awe, empathy, or curiosity, *any* emotion that you apply fits under a much larger umbrella, and it's one that speaks volumes about the true chasm between traditional advertising and the modern age. In short, there was one simple philosophical mindset that made this video stand out:

Value.

We offered *value* to the viewer.

It's a very simple concept, but one that many marketers don't fully understand. Traditional TV advertising was designed to be interruptive. It was shoved into the middle of your favorite show and felt very much like the price you had to pay to access the content that you really wanted. *Our approach flips that model on its head.* We create brand messaging that's inherently valuable, content that the audience actually *wants* to watch. And that value generates a massive response.

The reason for this is simple human nature. If a well-dressed stranger comes up to you on the street and flat out asks you for a dollar, you will likely be weirded out and back away, and you most certainly won't give him a dollar. If a colleague comes up to you the next day and she calls out to let you know you dropped your car keys, or puts a quarter in your parking meter or does something else that is selfless and *valuable* to you, you will immediately be more sympathetic to her. Because of this connection, you would have a much easier time striking up a conversation, perhaps recognizing that you have some common interests and maybe even start to form a quick little bond right there on the sidewalk. Then, when she realizes she's a buck short for her morning latte, how would you feel about offering her that dollar in your pocket?

Sure, you'd chip in for her latte. Or, at the very least, you would be far more inclined to. After all, she was nice and helpful to you first. She led with *value*.

The woman in this scenario may have worked a lot harder than the well-dressed stranger to separate you from your dollar, but in the end, she was successful. And he wasn't.

Our videos work the same way. We offer value without asking for anything up front. We walk up to strangers on the internet and say: "Hey, you a fan of John Cena? Have you seen this video where he pops out of a wall and surprises his biggest fans? You'd love it. Check it out!"

Once they've watched our content, this opens a dialogue and allows us to come back to them with other valuable content. We then identify the people who interact the most and are the most engaged, and only then, far down the funnel, do we ask them to part with their hard-earned dollars.

And they do. Because we led with *value*.

In Chapter 2, we talked about how the act of sharing is actually a selfish act. We showed that in most cases people share not out of the goodness of their heart, but rather for how it makes them look or feel. This connects to value and forms a hugely important lesson, one that should fundamentally change your entire strategy about how you create content.

Put simply: If you want people to share your content, it has to be about *them,* not about you.

This is a concept that has been proven time and time again over the past ten years. In fact, it is at the core of what has made my company successful, and the reason we have been able to produce over 60 viral hits over the past few years.

Yet 99 percent of brands don't use it.

How can that be?

Well, the simple explanation is that it runs counter to the traditional core premise of advertising that has been ingrained in marketers for the past 80 years.

The Concept of Advertising: A Walk Down Memory Lane

People often talk about how much simpler things were in the "good old days." In some cases, that may be just a case of selective memory, but in the world of advertising, it is most certainly true.

Before television was invented, radio was the prevalent electronic medium in the United States, and it had the country's full attention. Back in the 1930s and 40s, popular radio shows would reach tens of millions of listeners every week. Brands could "advertise," and put their message in front of all of those attentive listeners, just by writing a check to the radio station.

Take, for example, when General Mills, the cereal company, started sponsoring the popular radio show *The Lone Ranger* in 1941. At its peak, *The Lone Ranger* radio broadcast had 20 million weekly listeners, all of whom gathered around their radios three times a week to listen to the show. For a brand, this was as good as it gets, a highly attentive audience who had no other option but to listen to your advertising as the price of admission to the show they were passionate about. Brands were even positioned as the heroes in this equation. The voice of God would announce that this program was made possible by Cheerios cereal, so remember: kids, eat your Cheerios! That's about the best advertisement a brand can hope for.

The strength of advertising continued with the advent of television. In the early days of television, continuing all the way into the 1980s, only three major networks showed full-time, high-quality programming, and they were all funded by advertising. If you were watching TV and a commercial came on, you basically had three choices:

1. Sit and watch it.
2. Change the channel — likely to another commercial, because networks synchronized their breaks.
3. Turn off the TV and go do something else.

This era is often noted as the golden age of advertising, when television held the nation's attention, networks thrived, and brands with deep pockets reaped the benefits of increased sales and a growing customer base.

In the late 1970s, cable channels started to pop up and gave viewers more options, but these were funded by advertisers as well, with the exception of then-rare subscription services like HBO. This created more channels to the TV lineup where brands could run their commercials.

The 1990s brought hundreds of channels and the invention of the commercial-blocking TiVo, a massive sign of the doom to come for the advertising trade. But the ad industry was still too busy enjoying the highlife and reaping huge fees to notice, and so it simply marched on like everything was status quo.

And then the internet happened. In the early days, there was a lot more hype than substance; as with any new medium, it took some time to find its footing. For the first decade of the internet, advertising on the internet was basically a messy collection of search traffic and overhyped banner ads. That all changed in 2005 when YouTube was launched. This marked the beginning of a massive shift in consumer behavior.

The internet gave people options that they never had before, and most important for brands, most of those options were not tied directly to advertising.

As a young man in the marketing field, this was an extremely exciting time for me and all of my colleagues. Nobody knew exactly how, but it was clear that the internet was going to change the way that brands interacted with their customers. Yet, to my surprise, not everyone seemed quite so thrilled.

In those days, senior people in the advertising world talked about the internet like it was some back-alley marketing sideshow, a kind of novelty or a fun little add-on to the "real world" of television advertising.

Here's what they all missed: the internet fundamentally changed how people interact with content. The audience no longer had to sit back and watch whatever had been prescribed to them by some network executive at a time that's been designated by a marketing department. Viewers could begin to want to watch what they wanted, when they wanted it, and as the technology advanced, on whatever damned screen they preferred. "Television" was now truly being delivered on demand.

This means the internet also changed the rules of advertising. Forever. This is happening in all kinds of complicated ways across screens big and small, but the core truth seems pretty simple to me. For starters: When people don't have options, they will tolerate advertising. But when they do have options, they will try to avoid it.

It's not emotional, it's just another self-serving decision. Simply put, who would watch advertising if they didn't have to?

So if your strategy is to interrupt what people actually want to watch with something that they don't want to watch, you will not be very successful. It's that simple.

The Concept of Value

So how do we define the difference between advertising and this new online concept of value? In the simplest terms, an advertising approach involves trying to impart your message to an audience, regardless of whether they want to hear it or not. A value-based approach, on the other hand, is understanding what your audience wants and giving it to them.

Here's a very practical example: Let's say Home Depot posts content on YouTube, or sends content to existing customers that tells them how to make fixes around the house, like stopping a leaky faucet or cleaning dirt from the grout in a kitchen floor. It posts a detailed, step-by-step video guide to fixing all kinds of things that can save you money.

Home Depot hasn't tried to sell you anything, but it has given you something of tangible value. Turns out that by watching the Home Depot video, you were able to fix that drip instead of spending $200 on a plumber. So now when you need a snow shovel, you will be more likely to go to Home Depot for it because *you have an affinity for the brand that has already offered you value.*

Remember, in the old days of television, the grand bargain with the audience was simple: If they wanted to watch a show, they had to watch the advertising along with it. That was the deal. The brand gave value in sponsoring the program, which essentially gave the audience "free" content.

Today, that deal has been torn to shreds. Yes, there are still plenty of places that show traditional advertising, but there are increasingly more that don't, like HBO, Netflix, Hulu Plus . . . the list goes on. And the younger generation — those who grew up with subscription options and YouTube at their fingertips — they have zero patience for interruptive ads. Skip this ad in 3, 2, 1 . . . skipped.

The younger the viewer, the less tolerance for advertising interruption. I see this at home, as I have a son, Max, who is 10 and a daughter, Allie, who is 8. They're growing up in the internet age. They were swiping an iPad at age 2 and have never known a world where they had to sit through traditional advertising to watch the shows that they wanted to see. If a commercial does come on, they just pull up another screen.

Imagine if your total sales message is contained in that commercial break. How effective do you think that will be?

So how do you make people watch your commercials? Well, you make the commercials inherently valuable. You make them into spots that people *want* to watch. That's the new deal for the new era: If you want an audience to watch your message, you must give them value. That means the first question you should ask yourself is not "What do I want to say?" but rather *"What does my audience want to watch?"*

This boils down to three basic questions:

1. Who do you want to reach?
2. What would that audience consider to be hugely valuable?
3. How can you provide it to them?

If you can determine the answers to these questions, and deliver something of true value, the audience will love you for it. Then, maybe you can ask them for that dollar in their pocket . . .

Engaging People with Commercials They Would Normally Skip

To truly understand how to create valuable content, we must first learn how to distinguish it from others. So, how can we spot valuable content?

The best way we've found to measure how well content is being received — and therefore how valuable it is — is called the Engagement Rate. This is the standard by which we measure the *meaningful* impact that a social media page can have. It measures every consumer who directly interacted with a brand's content and expresses that as a percentage of how many people were *exposed* to it. This is an extremely valuable data point. Let's take a look at why it is so important.

In the golden age of television, brands would spend tens of millions of dollars on television advertising, yet most would attain very limited feedback on how that advertising was received. Let's say 10 million people watched an episode of a popular show like NBC's *Friends,* during which a brand ran an advertisement. Of those 10 million people, how many actually watched that commercial? There is no way of knowing or measuring that. Perhaps half of them instead went to the bathroom, grabbed a drink, or made a phone call — or DVRed through all of the ads. The truth is, the brand sponsor will never really know. Though Nielsen does limited ad testing, for the people who did actually watch the commercial, how impactful was it in terms of getting them to gravitate toward that brand over the long term and buy its products?

So how is digital advertising different?

For starters, most everything on digital media is measurable. The social networks have endless amounts of data, information on countless people, all updated in real time by billions and billions of active users. They follow us around everywhere we go. Every time someone clicks a button, it's recorded. Every time someone skips an ad, or stops their feed to look at something, or swipes up to make it disappear, all of those actions are logged and recorded by a vast array of servers powered by an ever-changing and evolving network of artificial intelligence, also known as the algorithm.

Sounds sci-fi and scary? Ask your iPhone, and Siri will probably give you a very clever answer. She is an algorithm too.

In fact, there is an argument to be made that we are all algorithms. Or at least we can be interpreted as such. In other words, if you have enough data points on anyone, you can actually predict their behavior better than their friends, their families, or even themselves.

Researchers at the University of Cambridge and Stanford University have developed a computer model that can judge someone's personality down to a very eerie level of accuracy, using nothing but the subject's Facebook activity. When they compared the results against friends and family, the patterns were startling: The algorithm predicted a person's personality traits better than any of the human participants.

The. Computer. Was. Better.

In fact, it was so much better that it needed only 10 Likes on Facebook to beat a work colleague, 70 to beat a roommate, and 150 to beat a parent or sibling. And to defeat a spouse, the one person who arguably knows you better than anyone in the world? To do that, the computer needed only 300 of your Likes on Facebook.

This means computers *will* replace humans in terms of practical personality analysis.

At Shareability, we've been living in this reality for years. Facebook is particularly apt at knowing people better than they know themselves, and because people have *chosen* to give that data up, Facebook can offer it up for those users who haven't diligently followed the privacy locks to anyone who wants to interpret it.

So back to the engagement rate. We believe it to be the simplest and the most readily available data point measuring valuable content. The engagement rate is a direct measure of how many times someone interacted with a piece of content they were exposed to.

Here's how it breaks down:

- One person swipes right past your ad and doesn't stop to look at it — 0 points.
- One person stops for 3 seconds or more — 1 view point.
- One person reacts with a Like, a frown or other emoji, or comments on or shares the ad — 1 engagement point.

To determine the engagement rate, you divide the number of engagement points by the number of view points. For example, if 100 people watch a video and 2 people engage with it, the engagement rate is 2/100, that is, 0.02, or 2 percent.

As you can see, just racking up views doesn't really mean much in and of itself. A lot of those views will always be people who stuck around for only 3 seconds and then moved on, and that's not going to have any real impact on your bottom line.

But those people who really leaned in to engage with your content, those who liked, commented on, or shared it, those people are valuable. People tend not to interact with content before they've had a chance to watch it for a period of time, and even then, they interact only if what they were watching prompted a real emotional response — if they actually *felt* something. That feeling is your invitation to a relationship. It's the door through which you are allowed to enter and ultimately approach them for conversion.

All this being said, here's a surprising but essential rule of thumb: A really good engagement rate for a brand is around 1 percent.

That sounds like a low number, but remember, we are talking about people who actively leaned in and *chose to engage with a commercial.* That's a big ask. How many Honda commercials on TV have made you want to reach out to Honda and say, "Good job"? How many have made you want to send those Honda ads to all of your friends so that they can see it too?

The 1 percent engagement rate rule of thumb is not made up out of thin air. It is measured and calculated from best-in-class performance. The leading benchmark of digital advertising work is done by *Ad Age,* a magazine born in Chicago in 1930, which is now a global media brand, publishing analysis, news, and data on marketing and media. They publish the Ad Age Viral Leaderboard, which lists the top performers in online content monthly.

The median engagement rate for the Ad Age Viral Leaderboard in 2017 was 0.87 percent. That means if an ad was seen by 1 million people, about 8,700 of them cared enough to like, share, or comment.

That's best in class. It's Toyota, Coca-Cola, Ford, and other corporate behemoths spending millions and millions to drive these results.

Just FYI: The Shareability median over the same time period was a 2.09 percent engagement rate — a 240 percent increase over the Ad Age Viral Leaderboard.

If you break all of this down even further and look at what we consider to be the holy grail of digital marketing, the number of *shares,* our 2017 campaigns were shared 550 percent more than all the other top 200 best-in-class videos from the Ad Age Viral Leaderboard.

Not bad for a little upstart based in an industrial garage.

Giving People Something to Smile About

Over the past few years, we've worked with dozens of major brands on creating shareable content that is valuable to their audiences, with some brand categories being easier to work with than others. One of the toughest we've faced is the wireless category — it seems that just about everybody dislikes their mobile-phone provider. So we knew that we had quite the challenge when we got our first assignment from Cricket Wireless.

Cricket had done research that showed a clear pattern. When consumers truly enjoyed a positive image of their brand, those consumers were much more likely to buy wireless plans from them. Our assignment from them was simple: Create content that makes Cricket more likable. Now that was a concept that excited us! Cricket had even created a tag line for their new approach: giving their customers "Something to Smile About."

This tag line is a perfect example of the value-based approach. As we know, social media can be a very negative place. Our experience and internal research show that when faced with constant negativity, people favor fun, lighthearted content that makes them smile. If a brand can deliver that smile, then they have not only triggered the shareable emotion of happiness, but they have also given the audience something of *value*. Because this piece of content brightened their day, they are now more likely to view the brand in a favorable light, therefore increasing the odds that they will prefer that brand over the competition.

So by focusing on shareable "smile" emotions like joy, gratitude, and admiration, we went to work.

We planned our first campaign for Cricket Wireless around Mother's Day, 2016. We wanted to create a hero video that paid homage to moms, but did so in an entertaining and amusing way that their kids would also enjoy. Our brain trust generated a hilarious idea that was a sendup on a hot topic of that moment — photobombing, where people would unexpectedly jump in and "bomb" the back of someone else's photo. From this, we created "PhotoMombing," a spoof video where moms who were feeling left out of their kids' lives took back their rightful place in their children's pictures. Because we focused on value, the video struck a chord with moms and kids alike, went on to accumulate over 10 million views, and increased Cricket's Facebook engagement by more than a factor of ten in one month. And that was just the beginning.

The next campaign featured John Cena, the one where he burst through the thin wall. This campaign was so successful that it became the first brand video in the history of YouTube to be on YouTube Ad Leaderboard three months in a row (after debuting at number one). In total, the video has driven over 80 million views and, more important, pushed their social channels to a 2.42 percent engagement rate.

Since then, we have created and launched 12 additional campaigns for Cricket that ranged from Santa giving Christmas gifts to underprivileged kids, to celebrating Hispanic heritage, to a smash sequel to the original John Cena video, which became the most shared ad in the world — all gathered under the creative thematic of "Something to Smile About." Again, it's all about giving value to the viewer.

These campaigns have completely transformed Cricket's status in the telecom industry. After the hit videos, the Google searches of Cricket Wireless soared over 700 percent, brand lift (an increase of interaction with customers) jumped over 500 percent, and their conversion rate to sale was over 300 percent higher from the videos than their normal web traffic. Over the past three years their engagement rate went from last place in the industry to first place — results that were truly something to smile about.

All because we focused on value.

Rule 4

Find Your Voice

Now that you understand value, the next step is to find your unique voice to communicate that value. Sometimes that can be a winding road.

When my partners and I founded Shareability in 2014, it wasn't called Shareability. We had originally named the company Contagious. Everyone who worked here loved that name. It had a certain swagger and was very much of the moment for an upstart. At that time, viral videos were all the rage, and we were making videos that were the most "contagious" on the internet, like little video viruses that spread across the web. We started receiving laudatory press for our work, and we thought we were going to take over the online world.

Then one day I was opening the mail. One curious-looking envelope turned out to be a lawsuit being served from a UK company. The issue was that they were named Contagious as well, and they demanded we change our name immediately—or they were taking us to court.

At first, we were outraged. Their business was nothing like ours. How dare they ask us to change our name?

Then we vowed to fight it. That lasted all of about four hours, when our lawyer informed us that not only would we would lose the lawsuit, we would lose a lot of money in the process.

We were crushed. It sounds silly now, but at the time it felt like our company was going to end. We sat around for days, talking about trying to find a new name, not knowing what to do. We were so desperate to cling to our edgy brand name that at one point we actually considered changing the spelling of Contagious to end with a "z."

Finally, we resigned ourselves to the fact that we would have to come up with a name — and that's when something interesting happened. When we started to whiteboard what our company represented, we realized that the name Contagious was actually somewhat limiting. Sure, it sounded cool, but it also carried some negative connotations, namely that of carrying something that would infect others. Also, it was directly related to the term "viral," which had been the buzzword in the marketing world for the prior two years, but was starting to feel a little tired. How would it look a year or two down the road?

This exercise allowed us to stop and think for the first time and really articulate what we stood for as a company. At the time, long before video on Facebook was widely used, the concept of "sharing" online was just starting to gain steam. Being "shareable" was similar to being contagious, but it was actually much truer to who we were. It carried a more positive connotation, and it spoke to an interconnected ecosystem on social media where people share content with their friends and family. What a powerful concept!

Sharing was much more personal than the idea of some virus that was running loose across the web. It encapsulated how we wanted to build the company, everything from sharing risk with our brand partners that hired us to craft forward-looking campaigns to sharing the upside with our employees.

There it was, right at the heart of our business philosophy. That new name became our voice: Shareability. A word that wasn't even in the dictionary at the time. Today, most dictionaries do include the word and define it as how shareable something is, particularly in an online context.

Fast-forward to four years later, and the term "viral" is so played out, it is almost like a dirty word in the online marketing space. Conversely, everyone is talking about building a shareable brand, and we are perfectly positioned for where the market is heading as we deliver shareability for some of the biggest brands and celebrities in the world. The celebrities themselves become brands, like individuals looking to create profiles online, as a brand is the accumulation of traits that distinguishes one company or individual from another.

I never thought I'd say this, but I am grateful we were sued because it forced us to find our true voice.

Going to School on Celebrities

There are valuable lessons to be learned from working with people who are in a position of notoriety (even if that is not your aspiration), or learning about how they do what they do. If nothing else, that process will offer you some unique perspectives.

Before I started Shareability, I worked with celebrities and athletes in branding. In my early days at The Marketing Arm in Dallas, a firm founded by entrepreneur Ray Clark, we represented over 100 professional athletes and negotiated their marketing deals — everyone from the Chicago Bulls' Scottie Pippen to the Green Bay Packers' Reggie White. When I founded my first company, called Converge, we worked with professional poker players, including World Series of Poker champions Chris Moneymaker and Johnny Chan. As the company evolved, we engineered a celebrity event model that led to us managing over 200 celebrity events with some of Hollywood's biggest names, like Jamie Foxx, Mariah Carey, 50 Cent, Miley Cyrus, and, yes, the Kardashians. At one point, we rented a

$20 million beach house in Malibu for the summer and threw 40 celebrity events in 60 days. It was insane.

Since then we've partnered with celebrities like Leonardo DiCaprio on building his foundation and Shawn Mendes on launching a new brand.

From all of that exposure to celebrities, I learned two things. Number one, never play poker against someone who has the equivalent of your annual salary in his pocket (that's a story for another time!). Number two, the celebrities with the most staying power all have one thing in common: they inherently understand their unique voice.

This is a truth that is well known in Hollywood. To see it in action, look no further than the three Hollywood Toms — Tom Cruise, Tom Hanks, and Tom Hiddleston. Despite having the same first name, there's no risk of audience confusion. When you see one of these guys on a billboard, you know what you're gonna get. Cruise will give you charm and action, Hanks will be a thought-provoking everyman, Hiddleston will be full of raffish mystery.

These three celebrities have all crafted themselves into brands with their movies and have marketed themselves accordingly. They have found their voices and have stayed true to who they are, and that allows them to break through the noise and to be bankable at the box office. The older two Toms have even managed to sway their brands as they have aged, shifting with the times to stay relevant to younger audiences.

Compare this to the influx of several Chrises in Hollywood. In what *Vanity Fair* dubbed "The Chris-ening of Hollywood," the business was invaded by handsome white actors named Chris that everyone kept confusing with one another — Chris Pine, Chris Pratt, Chris Hemsworth, and Chris Evans. It went so far that when Pine took the stage on *Saturday Night Live* to promote *Wonder Woman*, he burst into song, trying to delineate which Chris he actually was, standing in front of a picture of all four of them, singing, "I'm not *that* Chris. I look just like him, but I'm not *that* Chris." His star rose as he gave it voice, and people started to better tell the four apart.

With the rise of social media, the power to establish your voice has been gradually removed from the hands of studio marketers, publicists, and journalists. Suddenly, celebrities had the power to communicate directly with their fans in a way they never had before. This gave them the opportunity to further craft their own voice and to grow their own influence.

The celebrities who have done it best are the ones who clearly understand and deliver on their unique voice. Love her or loathe her, Kim Kardashian knows exactly who she is, and she delivers that "brand" to her followers every single day on social media. She walks the line of oozing sex and living the glamorous life of Hollywood royalty, while also coming across as a sweet mom and family girl who is quick to make fun of herself. It's no wonder that she has over 220 million followers across social media.

Or take Dwayne Johnson. The Rock is a real life superhero on Facebook and Instagram, posting insane workout videos, delivering inspirational messages, and showcasing wild adventures with his friends and fans. It is a nonstop fun experience that delivers positivity and community in a way that only the Rock can. As a result, he has become one of the top ten most-followed celebrities in the world.

But despite the obvious power of these new platforms, curiously, in the early days of social media, many celebrities were slow to embrace this new social explosion. Numerous Hollywood stars were actually advised that they were "above" social media and would somehow be cheapening their brand by interacting directly with their fan base. This proved to be bad advice. The celebrities who dove into social media in the early days have reaped huge rewards for their first-to-the-game advantage. Even more significant, those who didn't left a celebrity void in the market that allowed new voices to spring up and skyrocket to prominence.

This is what led to the birth of the social media star.

The Social Media Star

In the pre-internet days, celebrities were made the hard way. Actors, artists, and musicians would toil for years in obscurity, honing their craft and waiting for their big break in the form of a major record-label contract, a plum role in a studio film, or a guest spot on *Johnny Carson*. Hollywood was the kingmaker, and the studio, network, and record-label execs held immense power as to whom they would anoint as the next big thing. For a wannabe celebrity, there really wasn't an alternative path to achieving widespread fame and fortune. They had to grind it out in the Hollywood machine and hope for the best.

The internet blew this concept to smithereens. For the first time, everyday people had the power to broadcast their message with an unlimited pipeline. Those that did it really well could reach millions and millions of people and become a bona fide celebrity, all without having to be anointed by the Hollywood star-making machine. We entered an era when "digital influencers" were being created at warp speed, often leaping from their parents' basement to international fame and millions of subscribers in a matter of months.

Watching this happen in real time has given us an unprecedented view of how celebrity is created in the internet age. At Shareability, we've literally had a front-row seat and watched virtual unknowns become international megastars in the blink of an eye. Consequently, we can objectively judge why certain people have broken through the noise while countless others try and fail.

If you review the success stories, one theme becomes overwhelmingly clear and bears repeating: The most successful social media stars are the ones who clearly understand their own unique voice, and who use that voice to reach people across the digital universe.

One example of finding one's voice is Jay Shetty.

Today, Shetty is one of the biggest influencers in the world on Facebook, sort of a millennial version of Tony Robbins if you will, at least insomuch as he shares life-changing wisdom in a way that is relatable and entertaining. When Shetty launched his channel in 2016, very few people had even heard of him. But by 2018, he crossed the 18 million mark in number of followers and drove over 3 billion views, creating multi-million-dollar opportunities in the process.

How did he become so successful so fast? Like all good overnight success stories, it didn't happen overnight.

Growing up in London, Shetty was shy, introverted, and bullied. At the tender age of 16, he lost two of his best friends, one to a car accident, the other to gang violence. Fighting to straighten up and fly right, Shetty managed to get into business school and graduated with honors, but the corporate world was too constricting for the 22-year-old. This is when he took a monumental step — Jay Shetty traded his suits for robes, shaved his head, and traveled across India and Europe to live as a monk.

For three years, he studied ancient Eastern philosophies, fasting for days at a time, meditating for hours every day. Half his day was spent on personal growth, the other half on helping others. He worked to build sustainable villages in India and Europe for those in need and coached millennials across the globe on consciousness, well-being, and the meaning of success.

Upon returning to England, Shetty moved back in with his parents, penniless and, by Western standards, having already committed career suicide. His friends from business school were all in high-powered jobs, yet Shetty couldn't afford bus fare. But then something interesting happened. His old friends started inviting him to speak to their businesses, to bring into the business world some of that calm and consciousness he'd acquired from his travels. As it turned out, all of his old friends were under immense pressure every day, and they needed guidance and wisdom. This was something that Shetty had in abundance.

During this process, Shetty started making inspirational videos. Though they were low-key and came from a complete unknown, they had authenticity in spades. They reflected who Jay was and the insights he'd gathered from his unique experiences. In short, he was being true to himself.

This caught the eye of Ariana Huffington, who brought him to the *Huffington Post,* where Shetty quickly established a loyal following. Within a year, he founded his own video agency and began to grow his personal brand.

Now he is well on his way to 100 million followers, all of whom he helps in their daily lives. His content is friendly, easy to access, and most inviting, with titles like "If You're in a Long-Distance Relationship, Watch This" and "If You Need Direction, Watch This." In keeping with his personal constitution, he gives all of his content away for free (sponsors support his work). He is truly offering nothing but pure value to his followers, which is why he has amassed so many. What he receives in return is the most valuable commodity of all: their attention.

Another example of being true to your voice is Richard Williams, better known as Prince Ea (who we worked with on the video featuring his poem "I Just Sued the School System!!!"). Prince Ea is a speaker and a poet who creates mind-bending spoken-word pieces on topics ranging from education to racism and the environment. He is a spiritual man with love in his heart, who preaches understanding and compassion to millions of followers — but it wasn't always this way.

Growing up in a rough area of St. Louis, Missouri, Prince Ea dreamed of being a rapper. He wanted to gain respect and perform in front of thousands of adoring fans. After struggling with this pursuit for years, he attained some level of success and a few breakthrough moments, but he was always looking ahead, at the people who were doing "better" than he was, and trying to figure out why, so he could fight his way up the ladder. Frustrated, Prince Ea actually quit. He realized that the dream he was pursuing was making him miserable and that what he really wanted — what he was trying to find through his music career — was happiness. He didn't really want to be a hip-hop star, he just wanted to be *happy*.

This revelation made him look for alternative paths to happiness. This is where his education served him well. He had received a full scholarship from the University of Missouri–St. Louis and graduated magna cum laude, with a BA in anthropology. Now he started reading about spirituality, picking up every book he could find, devouring ancient and modern texts alike.

Through this process of self-reflection, he realized that he would never find true happiness through doing anything. He determined that the act of *doing* is not where happiness can be found; it's only in *being* that true joy and peace exist.

With this new outlook on life, and the itch for creative expression ingrained in his DNA, Prince Ea picked up the pen again. This time, it wasn't rap that came out on the page, but poetry — modern, edgy, and thought-provoking poetry, rooted firmly in the spoken-word tradition that was at the time merely an artsy fringe genre.

But the popularity of the genre didn't matter. Prince Ea was being true to himself, and something amazing happened: the audience responded. His spoken-word poems quickly eclipsed all the other work he had done, not just in terms of popularity and passive views but in terms of resonance. The audience loved what he was doing, they engaged with it, and they shared it, bringing him more and more followers.

Prince Ea always had the talent, but it wasn't until he discovered his true voice that his career really took off. He has now become a major digital influencer and found his own lane to travel in, one that makes it cool to be smart. He explains complex topics in a deeply personal yet universally applicable way that is emotional, intelligent, and of the moment.

Prince Ea and Jay Shetty have similarities in that they both focus on spirituality and a positive understanding of our world, but this is certainly not the only path to success. A crass, edgy, and profane voice can also do the job, as proven by Canadian Indian influencer Lilly Singh, also known as IISuperwomanII. Singh is all about conquering life and living it like a "Boss" (or "Bawse," as she would spell it).

Her unique voice packs a wallop because she presents a genuine attitude of "never back down," and because she is completely transparent about her views and values, taking on all comers by calling people out on their bullshit. She focuses primarily on empowering girls and young women, helping them to overcome fear at school, to challenge bullies, and to make their own way in a sometimes troubled world. She has branched out her message to take on bigoted lunkheads by sending up their ignorance in a raw, comical, and unvarnished way, with a voice that is irreverent, accessible, and entertaining. She tackles slices of injustice, bias, and self-doubt that pertain to her and her outlook on life, and her message, including a best-selling book, is resonating with an ever-growing audience.

One of her top videos is "A Geography Class for Racist People." It was spurred by a troll commenting on one of her posts, saying: "Go bak to ur country, you terrorist paki afghan indian muslim slut #MakeAmericGreatAgain" (with all kinds of typos and even "America" spelled incorrectly).

Rather than engaging in meaningless discourse, Singh took this opportunity to pause and speak directly to her audience about the two types of people who rise up when something horrible happens in the world — "People who don't let fear divide them, and instead choose to come together," as she says, and "racist idiots who don't deserve an internet connection."

She proceeds to literally take this particular racist idiot to school, saying, "I just don't like when people are bad at things. If you're gonna be racist, at least do it right." Standing in front of a world map, Singh mockingly delivers a geography class, speaking down to him as if addressing a 4-year-old, in language dripping in irony, with a few salty interludes mixed in. "It's probably been years since you've had the chance to use your passport, just like your penis," she says with a sly smile. "But don't worry, this time you'll actually take off."

She points out the distance between her actual home country, Canada, and his mis-agglomeration of countries he wants her exiled to, noting that "India, Pakistan, and Afghanistan are actually three separate countries, you silly American-Aussie-Brit."

The video is a master class in simplistic sketch comedy, with expertly timed pauses and witty dialogue delivered with exactly the right amount of zing. It also aims to deliver on a much loftier goal, that of shooting down the ugly face of misplaced American nationalism, while focusing on inclusion, compassion, and education.

This tone is 100 percent in line with the Singh brand, and her audience is eating it up. With 35 million followers and billions of views on her videos, Singh is not only on the *Forbes* list of highest-paid YouTube stars, but more significantly she has been named a UNICEF Goodwill Ambassador, an honor she holds in the highest regard.

The reason these influencers, along with many others, have achieved such immense success and amassed such huge followings is because they have all found their own unique voice. They speak to their audience in a way that is authentic and true to who they are.

Brands need to learn from them and to think the same way. While you can argue the validity of treating corporations as people in the legal arena, from a marketing standpoint it's the only path forward. Brands need to think of themselves as people. They need to become unique, identifiable, definable. They need to have a clear and distinctive voice that stands out in the crowd of marketing madness, helps them become singular and recognizable, and ultimately causes their message to break through the noise.

Your Philosophy Is Your Voice

The leap from a personality archetype to a brand archetype is not completely linear, but it's also not a moon launch. In the martini days of traditional advertising, Madison Avenue often defined brand philosophy and told the brands what to think. Ad agencies were paid millions of dollars to come up with slogans that supposedly encapsulated the essence of a brand in only a few words. Many of those slogans were marketing tools that worked so well, they became part of the public consciousness, but that doesn't mean they truly defined the brand's philosophy.

For example:

- Tastes Great, Less Filling — Miller Lite
- Finger Lickin' Good — Kentucky Fried Chicken
- Don't Leave Home Without It — American Express

Note how these slogans simply help define a product. "Finger Lickin' Good" tells you that KFC is so yummy, you'll want to lick every last bit of fried chicken off your fingers — but there's no actual information about the brand or what it stands for. All it says is "we have delicious chicken." That worked really well for over

50 years, but in 2011 reality finally caught up with the fast-food chain. KFC dropped their famous catch phrase and started searching for new messaging, something that fit with the times. As of this writing, they are still looking.

This is not to say that catch phrases are outdated. They can still work by ingraining themselves in the zeitgeist, but today catch phrases cannot be only about defining a product. They must define the *philosophy* of the brand. Consumers are increasingly aware of what a brand stands for, and this core of a brand influences where they take their business more than ever before. Brands that are seen as having integrity and a social conscience are drawing far more customer attention than those that are simply product-centric.

Sometimes a great slogan *can* also encapsulate the spirit and essence of a brand. For example:

- Just Do It! — Nike
- Because You're Worth It — L'Oréal
- Think Different — Apple

Catch phrases like these convey a higher purpose. These can be used to build an online narrative and marketing strategy because they tell everyone who the brand is on an emotional and value-based level, rather than just a product level.

Note how none of these slogans even talk about, or point to, any specific product or product attribute. "Just Do It!" might just as well have been a slogan for a diaper brand, or pet food, or a skydiving school. This suggestion sounds silly now only because the slogan is so intrinsically tied to Nike in our minds that we can't see it any other way. These three simple words, capped off by an exclamation point, encapsulate a spirit of driving forward, of pushing yourself to the limit, of going for it, whatever "it" may be. The slogan tells you what the brand stands for and serves as a spiritual call to arms that makes you feel good about yourself for choosing this brand. What it doesn't do is say anything about shoes.

Likewise, "Because You're Worth It" doesn't speak to any specific product, but rather to a value. It lets you know that this is the brand you choose when you want to spoil or reward yourself, that this is the top of the line in the category, whatever that category may be, and that by choosing this brand, you are giving yourself a pat on the back and making yourself feel good — because you deserve it. That said, in the age of social awakening and social consciousness, it will be interesting to see how long this particular slogan continues to work for L'Oréal.

"Think Different" is a classic catch phrase that encapsulates the philosophy of Apple and has a very strong connection to Steve Jobs in the minds of customers. The slogan works because it's pure and came from who they are. It is linked to a specific watershed moment in Apple's history that helped define not just the young upstart brand at the time, but the entire future of home computing and, to no small degree, the mobile media revolution that enabled me to write this book in the first place.

This all harks back to 1997, the year Steve Jobs returned to Apple after having been exiled from the company he had helped create years earlier. His return sparked a much-needed and painful change. An entirely new board of directors was brought in, new products were announced, old product lines were cut, and a licensing deal with Microsoft settled a long-running legal dispute, allowing Jobs to turn his eye to marketing.

Apple's advertising agency, BBDO, came up with the slogan "We're back," which everyone loved — everyone except Jobs. He said the slogan was stupid because Apple wasn't back. He was right. They weren't back, not by a long shot. They needed something to help them *get* back.

Jobs invited other agencies to pitch ideas. One of them was Chiat/Day, the team behind Apple's famous "1984" commercial that launched the first Macintosh personal computer. They came back with the core concept behind the "Think Different" campaign. Jobs called it brilliant because he recognized it as being core to the company—what they used to stand for and what they should stand for again.

When the first Mac was introduced, the idea of a personal computer was pretty much far-fetched, unrealistic sci-fi nonsense. Computers were housed in warehouses, and only large corporations could afford them. Have one on your desk at home? Apple was clearly crazy.

Well, here's to the crazy ones. The philosophy of thinking differently, or "Think Different," as the grammatically incorrect campaign was named, had been a core value for Apple since the very beginning. When they initially lost Jobs, the company lost sight of that. They started licensing their software, farming out their hardware, and making dull gray boxes that looked like everyone else's. They lost their distinctive voice. With Jobs back at the helm and in the midst of the "Think Different" campaign, they would launch the new iMac line and the iBook laptop, seeing both profits and the stock price soar. It was the comeback story of the century, and it was all because the company returned to its true voice.

The best way to find your true voice is to strip away the gloss and sheen and return to whatever it was that made you think your business was a good idea in the first place, like we did at Shareability, and like Apple did. But make sure you are telling the truth.

To test this truth, we have developed four key steps based on our experience to help brands through this transition. If you're struggling with finding your voice, these steps should serve as a roadmap of sorts, or at least guideposts.

1. Do basic research to find out who you are *not.*

Normally, you would do market research to find out *what you can sell.* In this case, you are doing market research to find out *who you are.* This sounds a bit overwhelming, but there's a trick you can employ to circumvent the extremely broad nature of the question, and to help you home in on the truth.

You ask people who they think you are and what you should be doing, in terms of services, products, ventures, what have you. In truth, their answers won't be as interesting or as telling as *your reaction to them.* Remember, you are looking for *your* truth, not the truth of others. That means, for example, that if you are a marketing company like Shareability and someone says, "You should become an advertising agency and compete with everyone making million-dollar TV commercials because you would be really good at it!," that comment might make your skin crawl.

That's where you pause. Why did that just happen?

You are not looking for the truth in what people say, only the truth in how that makes you *feel.* If half the people you ask tell you to compete with advertising agencies, but your instincts are screaming that this is the wrong path, that the agency model is dying, that TV commercials are the past and digital communication is the future, then you would be foolish to listen to the market research.

As our chief creative officer would say: "Statistics is the science that can tell you a person who is standing with one foot in a fire pit and the other in a block of ice is — on the average — doing great."

Of course they are not. They are literally screaming in great pain from the fire and the ice but no spreadsheet or pie chart will ever be able to display these real emotions. That's because humans are complex machines and everything we do is interconnected, not least of which is all your passion and your success. Remember, your passion is key. That doesn't mean that you will automatically succeed at any-thing you are passionate about, but at least it means you have a head start and a fighting chance.

But, you ask, what if I'm not a passionate person? Well, then you don't know yourself very well. Everyone is passionate about some-thing. It's simply in our DNA. You need to figure out what *aspect* of your business you are passionate about. It probably won't be "be-coming successful" or "making lots of money" or any such arbitrary and generic response. It will be oddly specific, deeply personal, and unique to you and your business in some very interconnected way.

For me, I love packaging. The idea of taking a slice of this, a hint of that, layered on a thick base of something else, combined in a new and unique way that tells a *story* that makes everyone excited the minute they hear it—that's where my true passion lies. I have be-grudgingly come to realize this is probably because I'm a storyteller. Initially I shunned the idea. It sounded soft and artsy, and lacking in profit potential, but then I realized that story is everything. It's in the story of their packaging and positioning that companies like Snap-chat, Airbnb, and Beats can be valued in the billions of dollars. It has nothing to do with detailed financials or even profit margins—it's all in the storytelling. That is the high-wire game that I am inexpli-cably drawn to, and thinking about the packaging and positioning of Shareability is where I can add real value to the company.

So who do you ask for your research? Well, anyone really. Start by asking friends, family, and coworkers. Read up on other companies that are like yours, or very unlike yours, and see if you can find some consensus on where you fit. The heart of this exercise is to pro-vide you with enough time and direction so that you can hear your own inner truth. Listen to the little voice that tells you where to go, and use the court of public opinion as guardrails to tell you where *not* to go.

2. Look at your competitors for opportunities.

Researching and understanding the voices that are already prevalent in your industry is a productive exercise to help you find your unique position. The trick is to find a market gap for a voice that aligns with something you believe in. That's where the sweet spot lives.

An example of this is Jessica Alba and The Honest Company. Early in her career, Alba made a name for herself as the star of the television hit *Dark Angel* and in hit films including *Fantastic Four, Sin City,* and *Valentine's Day.* Her persona and voice at the time were all about mystery and Hollywood glamour. That all changed in 2007, when she found she was pregnant with her first child. Her parental instincts kicked in, and she began researching all the things that she would need to know to be a successful mom.

One of the first books she read was *Healthy Child Healthy World,* by Christopher Gavigan, and it had a profound impact on her. The book served as a textbook for Alba on the dangers of toxic chemicals in baby products and the connection of these chemicals to various illnesses. As a child, she herself had experienced asthma and allergy-related illness; she was convinced there had to be a connection.

She was outraged to find out that regulatory systems were failing consumers and that manufacturers were allowed to put untested, toxic chemicals in products like baby shampoo and diapers in order to provide fragrance. She then scoured the market for "clean" products that wouldn't put her baby at risk. What she found depressed her — there were very few products that were actually clean, and the exceptions were of poor quality or very expensive.

Out of this personal inner-voice journey, Alba made a life-changing move. She decided to become the voice for moms who demanded high-quality, safe, and affordable products for their children. She launched The Honest Company to do just that. It took several years to hone the business plan and secure the initial funding, during which time Alba had a second child. But in 2012, the company was up and running. It was working because it had a very unique voice, that of a brand that listens to parents and keeps their kids safe. The company skyrocketed because of that, and by 2015, its valuation had reached $1.7 billion. *

This process happened naturally for Alba, but you can do it much more deliberately. The first step is to take a deep look at the industry or category that you want to enter and then carefully study the voice of all of the major players in it. Try to boil down each voice into a few words and then write down what they stand for. Then look at all of

* The Honest Company webpage via honest.com.

your competitors as a whole, and think about how they are different and how they are the same. Are there any major holes in the market that come to mind? Is there room for a more conscientious brand? An edgier one? One that appeals directly to a specific demographic? Where are the opportunities? If you can pinpoint and identify an opportunity that aligns with something you are passionate about, like Alba did, then you are off to the races.

Finding your own voice can also mean making a change in your career or life path. My partner and a cofounder of Shareability, Nick Reed, is a perfect example of this.

Nick came up through the Hollywood ranks at International Creative Management (ICM), one of the industry's top talent agencies. He started out as an agent's assistant, was promoted to agent, and then rose to become head of the motion-picture literary department at ICM. He represented some of the top film directors and writers in the business, including Jay Roach (the Austin Powers and Meet the Parents series), Antoine Fuqua (*Training Day*) and Peter Morgan (*Frost/Nixon*), and put together hit movies such as *Bridget Jones's Diary*.

His days were long, and weekends offered no reprieve. There seems to be a dictum in the agency business that if you don't work a full day on Sunday, don't bother showing up on Monday because someone else will have your job. Despite the pressures, Nick loved representing some of the most talented people in the business and bringing their work to the big screen, and he forged ahead.

But over the years, the agency game began to change. Big agencies had to get bigger to compete, and acquisitions became the order of the day. Other agencies were constantly trying to poach his clients. So not only was Nick working with his clients, he was dealing with personnel issues, attacks from competitors, and intra-agency power grabs. One day, he sat back and looked at what he had achieved and what he wanted out of his career.

Yes, he had worked with the best filmmakers and biggest movie stars. Inasmuch as the job required creativity, much of his time was spent deal making and problem solving. He wasn't actually telling the stories, he was facilitating them. So, in 2010, he took a leap into the unknown and left ICM to pursue his own creative avenues. He wanted to do something that moved him, something that was good for his soul.

Soon after, he met Alice Herz-Sommer. She had the most amazing story he had heard in years. She was the world's oldest living Holocaust survivor, at 107 years old, with a unique story of survival and an outlook on life that moved Nick. An accomplished pianist, she was sent to the Theresienstadt concentration camp with her 6-year-old son. To endure and maintain her sanity, she turned to music. She performed more than 100 concerts inside the concentration camp, helping others maintain their sense of sanity as well.

Never mind the commercial prospects, Nick had to film her story. He convinced his longtime friend, documentarian Malcolm Clarke, to work with him on the film. Using his own money with Malcolm and working pro bono, they made a short film titled *The Lady in Number Six: How Music Saved My Life,* about how music, laughter, and optimism can lead to human triumph over the most trying circumstances.

Nick poured all of his know-how into the making of the film and its marketing, so that Alice's story would be heard. He also discovered something about himself, that he in fact needed to be creative to be happy. He brought this with him to Shareability.

To promote the film, we put together easily shareable clips from the film's footage, and then aggressively pushed those gems out to bloggers and influencers. The resulting reach was so vast and the media attention so wide that it gained the attention of Academy Award voters, who nominated the film for an Oscar.

After the nomination, we continued to build the community and awareness around the film. The combination of a wonderful film and its positive message helped push the film over the top. On Oscar night, *The Lady in Number Six: How Music Saved My Life* won the Oscar for Best Documentary Short Subject. Sadly, Alice died, at 109, a week before the ceremony. However, she lived to see her story impact so many people, as well as help Nick, who had won an Oscar for his first film, find his own voice.

3. Formulate and hone your mission statement.

This may seem self-aggrandizing, but at Shareability we honestly believe that the path to finding your mission statement lies in figuring out what's shareable about your brand. Why would anyone want to tell their friends about you? Why would they share your story?

This is surprisingly applicable to even the dullest of businesses. Even a coat-hanger manufacturer has a story worth telling, you just have to dig deep enough to find it. It's an exercise in finding the truth at the heart of the company and then romanticizing it to the hilt.

The bottom line is this: *If a brand is doing something right, then it has a core value or asset that will cause people to respond.* Something exists at the heart of the brand that defines it, and makes it unique. The key here is that this essence is not necessarily a selling point, but a core philosophy that makes the brand true to itself, that gives it a voice.

Take a look at the clothing brand Patagonia. They grew out of a small company that made tools for mountain climbers. They still do, but now they also make clothes for skiing, snowboarding, surfing, fly-fishing, paddling, trail running, and anyone who just wants to feel snug sitting in an outdoor café on a cool fall day. What they don't make is motorcycle jackets, racing gloves, or team jerseys. They make products for the quiet sports, practiced in the outdoors, with a focus on individual achievement.

Their values still reflect the minimalist style of their roots, and their designs are always coming from a place of simplicity and utility. This love of the outdoors, the wild, is what has led them to take part in the fight to preserve our wildlife, flora and fauna alike. They work hard to minimize the pollution created by manufacturing, and they donate time, energy, and a percentage of their sales revenue directly to grassroots environmental groups all over the world.

Staying true to these core values, and making high-quality products, means they can command a premium from their customers. People are willing to pay extra for this kind of corporate integrity.

This truth at the center of the company has been boiled down to a mission statement that says Patagonia exists to "build the best product, cause no unnecessary harm, and use business practices to inspire and implement solutions to the environmental crisis." Not bad for a company that's been in business 30-plus years and is now doing over $200 million in revenue every year.

4. Above all, be honest.

The internet has a finely tuned bullshit detector that operates at warp speed. Unlike the days of television advertising, when people had to write letters to a company about bad or misleading slogans or wait until a newspaper wrote about it, today people can comment immediately — and boy, do they. Any whiff of inauthenticity in your voice or your message will blow up in your face at the speed of a Reddit thread.

Granted, this may be on a small scale for you or for a small brand, but consider what happens to a large brand when it posts something that seems inauthentic. A case in point is Pepsi's campaign with Kendall Jenner.

Long ago, Coca-Cola was the dominant soft drink. It was "the real thing." When Pepsi came along, they had to figure out a way to separate and distinguish themselves from Coke, to show that they were the new cola on the block. They came up with "the choice of a new generation," and Pepsi pursued the youth market with amazing success.

But Pepsi has lately lost touch with the new generation. Pepsi produced an ad in 2017 that featured a white celebrity defusing a protest march with a Pepsi. In the ad, protesters are holding signs that read "Join the Conversation," while surrounded by police. In the final scene, Kendall Jenner hands a police officer a Pepsi, ending the confrontation and causing the protesters to applaud.* The tone-deaf ad uses images related to Black Lives Matter, a movement

protesting police brutality, in order to sell its soda.

This isn't to say a brand can't be edgy, witty, or sardonic. It can, as long as it rings true. Taco Bell has done a terrific job with its irreverent social media campaign aimed at millennials. When Taco Bell set out to announce its home delivery app, it went dark on social

---

* "Live for Now Moments Anthem," Pepsi commercial originally televised April 2017.

media. On every platform, over a black screen with white letters, it wrote: "Taco Bell isn't on Twitter," or "Taco Bell isn't on Facebook. It's #OnlyInTheApp."

Everything Taco Bell does in its social media marketing stays true to its appeal to millennials. When it discovered there was no emoji for a taco, Taco Bell started a petition on change.org. After 33,000 people signed, a taco emoji was created. Taco Bell took things a step further, creating the Taco Emoji Engine.

Undoubtedly, Taco Bell's marketing team carefully considers and plots its strategy. But it doesn't feel that way, because with each step, the brand maintains its authenticity, which appeals to its target-market base.

So when you find your voice, make sure it is very true to your brand, to who you are, and to the core idea that caused you to put so much time and effort into it in the first place. That honesty will make all the difference as to whether your voice is ultimately heard.

Rule 5

Crush the Headline

From the early days of Shareability, we've always had a very simple and ironclad rule — if you don't have a knock-out headline, well, you don't have a video.

This started in our YouTube days, where a large part of our distribution strategy was to have our videos noticed and then written up by publications around the world. In order to make that happen, the videos needed to be headline-worthy from a journalistic point of view. While we don't focus on publications for PR nearly as much these days, the same original mantra translates beautifully to the current digital landscape, helping to hone the clarity and specificity of our campaigns. I can't tell you how many times I've repeated this around the office: "If you don't have a killer headline, you don't have a video."

Newspapers understood this concept before the internet even existed. "Headless Body in Topless Bar" is a classic *New York Post* headline. Known for its puns and wordplay, the *Post* has been running saucy, attention-grabbing headlines for decades. The paper hopes that a fun headline will make you want to buy the paper and read the story, and for years, it was also trying to out-headline the other New York City daily tabloids.

More traditional newspapers, like the *New York Times* and the *Wall Street Journal,* use headlines differently, keeping them much more focused on the content of the story. This results in news-driven headlines, like "Storm Gathers Strength as It Nears Florida" or "Passenger Is Dragged from Overbooked Flight." For a more important story, these papers will increase the size of the font, creating a banner headline, but they won't resort to *New York Post*–type puns for fear of losing credibility. It's a delicate balance between credibility and audience attention, but the bottom line is that if you are a newspaper, headlines matter.

Yet, ironically, it seems that for many agencies and traditional content creators, the headline of a video is nothing more than an afterthought. In my opinion, they could learn a thing or two from newspapers. In short, I'm here to tell you that if your headline is an afterthought, then your video will be an afterthought as well.

In a world where people are bombarded on a daily basis by thousands of channels and millions of messages, only the most pointed messages break through. To be noticed at all, you need to command attention. Sure, you need to be unique and memorable, but most important, your message must be easy to understand. *If it takes more than one sentence or phrase to grab people's attention, they will have already moved on.*

When you're scrolling through social media, your initial attention span is a matter of milliseconds. That's why videos work so well in general, because they *move* as you swipe past them. The movement itself causes your brain to focus. It's a simple animal instinct. We are genetically predisposed to notice movement, because anything that moves can be a threat, or food. Our brains gravitate toward the moving object or image, lingering longer than they would for anything that is static; as a creator, that buys you a few precious moments when people will pay attention and watch.

Now, to get someone to actually stop and watch a video beyond those first few seconds, two things need to happen simultaneously — *the concept needs to grab their attention AND they need to understand it immediately.*

If it doesn't grab their attention, they will simply be on to the next post.

If they don't immediately understand what it is, they will give up and move on.

Through this lens, the best idea in the world is completely worthless without the right packaging, and again, the headline is the key to packaging content on social platforms.

In this context, the concept of a headline is twofold: Philosophical and Tactical. In this chapter, we'll cover both concepts, starting with the four-step process of how Shareability thinks about headlines. The first two are more philosophical, the second two more tactical. Master them all, and you too can crush your headlines.

1. Nail the "Get It" Factor

I'm going to talk about the "Get It" Factor first, because I think this mindset is the most important. This is the "understand it immediately" part that I mentioned above. For a video to be successful on social media, the viewer must "get it" in the first few seconds. The video *must* state its purpose immediately.

If you start on a slow fade into a lovely landscape and some elegant imagery of trees with a flaring orange sun setting in the background, I have no idea what I'm watching. It could be a documentary about Cardiff or a Honda commercial. Because the first few seconds don't tell me what I'm watching, it is very unlikely that I'm going to stick around to find out. I have better things to do, like checking out the cute otter in the next video — which is juggling rocks! Look at that guy go . . .

And just like that, your video is gone. I may have stuck around for 3.1 seconds, just long enough to count as a view on Facebook, but that's not going to help you in the long run. You didn't hook me, and I still have no idea what your video was about. I didn't get it, so I won't be liking or sharing your video.

This is why the "Get It" Factor is so important. It's a combination of the actual headline, the thumbnail (if I'm not set to autoplay), and the first few seconds of the video, all working in full concert to tell a crystal-clear story. With the din of constant noise coming from all corners of the internet, the reality is that people aren't going to watch something that doesn't strike a chord with them in a matter of seconds. And if they don't *get it,* they won't care.

When one of our creatives pitches an idea to the team, my first question is always the same: "What's the headline?" This is not a literal question. I'm not asking them to outline the actual copy that will be placed next to the video when it is launched. I'm asking: *"What is the core shareable concept of the video?"* I'm asking them to sum up that concept in one short sentence, just like a headline. If it takes three sentences to explain the idea, I shake my head and tell them to go back to the drawing board, because they don't have a shareable idea.

This simple insight has had as great an impact on our success as any other.

A clear example of this that we touched on earlier was when we were looking for a shareable concept to help promote the Olympic Channel. The Olympic Games are on everyone's mind for a few short weeks every other year, when the Winter and Summer Games are in full swing. But between the games, the public is focusing on other things, and only the real hard-core Olympic junkies are following the ins and outs of the various sports and the athletes' progress. The Olympic Channel is built to bridge that gap as the home for all things

Olympic in between the games and to remind people of the wonderful memories of those games, which live forever.

As we started exploring different themes and concepts for the
Olympic Games, we had a number of worthy and compelling ideas.
There was a concept for a spoken-word piece centered on the athletes' grueling training regimens. There was a humor piece about
superstar athletes who were not good at everyday things like cooking or yard work. And we also had an idea for a global anthem being
performed by big-name musicians.

But in the end, there was one simple idea that everyone jumped
on because it was by far the simplest and most impactful of all: Baby
Olympics. *

* "If Cute Babies Competed in the Olympic Games," published on YouTube April
13, 2017, from the Olympic Channel.

Here's the one-line pitch: "What if babies competed in the Olympic Games?"

Now that's a great headline! The concept was easy to grasp and visualize. Plus it came with a baked-in "Get It" Factor. There was no way you would ever scroll past this and not *get it*. This is why the headline tested so high in our internal vetting and why we were so confident it would be imminently shareable.

Of course, it took a few rounds to convince the Olympic Channel that this was the idea they should endorse. It was certainly uncharted territory for them, as they tended to focus on the games as a celebration of human athletic excellence. Now, hundreds of millions of views later, it has become one of the most successful promotions they've ever done — all because of the inherent "Get It" Factor of the headline.

When you can combine that "Get It" Factor with one of the shareable emotions — happiness, awe, empathy, curiosity, or surprise — all sorts of interesting things happen. It's traditional wisdom that when you see a video online, watch the full video, and enjoy it enough, you will feel compelled to share it with your friends. Our linear way of thinking would have all of these things happen in that order, but in the real world, this is not the progression. We have found a fascinating phenomenon in our research that most people aren't aware of: As soon as the "Get It" Factor hits a shareable emotion, people will immediately share the video, even if they are only 15 or 30 seconds in. People don't even wait for, or even need to watch, the rest of the video before they share. They blast it to all their friends and followers right there and then, meaning that a substantial percentage of people share videos *before* they've even watched them. If that's not the most compelling reason to nail the "Get It" Factor, I don't know what is.

2. Think Like a Journalist

When we first started Shareability in 2014 (when it was still called Contagious), we specialized in brand videos going viral on YouTube. At the time, there was far less content and noise on the platform than there is today, but even so, the odds of reaching a large audience and "going viral" were very heavily stacked against you. What we learned early on is that there was no quicker way to rise up the YouTube algorithm than to receive coverage of your video in prominent digital news outlets and blogs. Journalists would write articles about newsworthy (meaning shareable) videos, and these articles would in turn drive tens or hundreds of thousands of viewers to your video in rapid fashion. The more articles written about you, the faster your video rose.

This was basically the ultimate hack to rocket up the video charts, in some cases all the way to the front page of YouTube. And we became really proficient at it. If you look at our early hits, you'll see that they have large numbers of digital articles. Our video featuring "The Apparently Kid" for Freshpet generated dozens of articles. "The Dangers of Selfie Stick Abuse" for Pepsi and Pizza Hut had hundreds. And when we distributed the "Kobe vs. Messi" ad (created by Crispin Porter) in 2014 for Turkish Airlines, we secured over 2,000 articles.

The reason that we were so successful at having our videos covered is that we learned to think like journalists. This took two distinct forms: First, we considered videos that were either topical or of the moment in some way. (I'll go into much more depth on this thought process in the next chapter.) Second, and every bit as important, we considered the idea of the headline *from a journalistic point of view.* I'm not trying to imply that we ever engaged in actual journalism; rather, we took the time to try to understand how the journalists writing about our campaigns might *think*. We actively put ourselves into the shoes of the people writing these articles and asked the key question from their perspective: "What do *I* want out of this?"

Remember, everyone is selfish. They are focused on what benefits *them,* not you.

So what does a journalist for an outlet like Mashable or the *Huffington Post* want? It's pretty simple. They want an article that is going to be clicked on as many times as possible and widely read, which helps raise their own profile (and earning potential) as a writer and in turn attracts more readers to Mashable and the *Huff Po,* which ultimately sells more advertising.

If we can deliver a story that becomes an article that is attention grabbing and something that the people surfing the internet would want to read about, then the journalist is far more likely to write an article about our video. We are providing *value,* and they are receiving value in return. But journalists see hundreds or even thousands of potential stories every day, so why are they going to pick yours? Because you've done the hard work for them by delivering a shareable story on a silver platter that they can run with right away.

Let me give you an example. In 2014, we were approached by Sony Studios to help promote their upcoming film *Spider-Man 2*. This was one of the most successful movie franchises of all time, but the Spider-Man brand had started losing resonance with a younger audience. We were brought in to make the brand more relevant, particularly through our YouTube expertise.

It was a dream assignment for us to work on one of the biggest movies of the year, but it also presented a unique challenge. The Spider-Man brand is extremely well known throughout the world, and the studio was going to be spending hundreds of millions of dollars to market the film globally. Our YouTube campaign was nothing more than a rounding error in the budget of this tsunami of global promotion. Because of this massive marketing push, the film was destined to be a force at the box office, meaning it was already going to be covered in essentially every entertainment outlet in the world, from every angle. How could our little campaign break through all that noise and actually make a difference?

We knew that we needed to craft a narrative that would be written up in the right places to catch the eye of the internet, a truly new and fresh angle that people who are tired of standard movie marketing would gravitate toward, something that felt of the moment, of the internet. In order to execute that, we needed a journalist-friendly headline around a pop-culture conversation driven by young people on social media.

Tall order.

At the time, parkour was all the rage online. Parkour is the art of moving rapidly through an area, negotiating obstacles by running, jumping, and climbing, often using urban elements such as walls, railings, and rooftops to help create a sense of fluid movement. It's a mix of gymnastics, acrobatics, and street art, named after the French *parcours,* meaning "route" or "course." Parkour videos were blowing up on YouTube, with daredevils running, jumping, and flipping their way off of buildings, cars, and anything else as they flew through city streets.

Parkour also had a very loyal following of young people, and a few athletes were emerging as full-blown YouTube stars. One of those athletes was Ronnie Shalvis, a young guy from Salt Lake City, Utah, whose parkour videos were landing millions of views. Our team came up with the idea of partnering with Shalvis and putting him in the Spider-Man suit to create an epic parkour video. *

In the beginning of the video, Spider-Man is chasing down a crim

---

* "The Amazing Spider-Man Parkour" published on YouTube April 29, 2014, from Ronnie Street Stunts.

inal when he suddenly loses the ability to shoot webs and therefore crashes to the ground. Does he give up? No! Instead of riding his webs, he uses the latest parkour techniques in a way that only Ronnie Shalvis could, all captured in a cinematic style that managed to feel authentic yet somewhat homespun. The video was filmed in a way that was consistent with the popular parkour films of the time, with limited narrative and a heavy focus on the various tricks and flips that Shalvis performed. Young viewers love this attention to detail and watch these films so that they can learn and replicate the parkour techniques. It ended, in keeping with the character, with the police arriving to find that the bad guy had already been apprehended and Spider-Man was off to his next mission of justice.

All of this made for a compelling video around a hot topic for young people, but the key element was in the headlines that the journalists would write. As we were honing the concept, the team crafted a fun headline: "It's not Peter Parker, it's Peter Parkour." This was old-school wordplay with a modern twist that would have every journalist salivating, in effect doing half their work for them. It also happens to be the type of headline the internet would love — and it did. The video roared to the front page of YouTube, amassing over 15 million views on the main post and tens of millions more through rips and re-uploads across the web. It also drove hundreds of articles around the world, including our primary target, Mashable, where veteran journalist T. L. Stanley wrote "Can't Wait for 'The Amazing Spider-Man 2'? Check Out Peter Parkour."

The story was simple, and Stanley's article spells it out well: "What if Spider-Man runs out of the silky strong web that spits from his wrists? How will the high-flying superhero impress his girlfriend, thwart bad guys and save New York City? With his own two feet, obviously. He's Peter Parker, after all. Or, rather, make that Peter Parkour."

We couldn't have written it better ourselves.

Another example is a video we did for Happy Socks, a Swedish company that makes colorful socks. We celebrated their out-of-the-box thinking by creating an out-of-the-box idea with a catchy headline title: "Snowboarding In The Clouds."

What an amazing headline!

This idea came from Shareability's founding partner Cameron Manwaring, who had been involved with a lot of the early devin-supertramp videos. The basic concept is exactly how it sounds: we were going to tow a snowboarder on a 200-foot line behind a helicopter and have him effortlessly glide on top of the clouds. Four years later, it still is one of the coolest and most ambitious ideas that we've ever dared to execute. We were extremely bullish on the concept, as the powerful simplicity and visual appeal of the headline made it a sure thing to break through the noise and soar up the YouTube charts. We even partnered with a millionaire daredevil by the name of Adrian "Wildman" Cenni to perform the stunt and also help bankroll the steep cost of making the video happen. Everything was in place.

Until we actually tried to execute the video.

This concept had never been attempted before, and we quickly found out why. It was difficult and expensive to the point of being nearly impossible. We had visualized the rider gliding effortlessly and cutting through soft, fluffy clouds like a knife through butter, but once we had Wildman in the air, we realized the sobering truth: We were filming a guy dangling helplessly from a rope, not a snowboarder gliding across the friendly skies.

The sheer physics made this idea a nightmare. The grace of snowboarding comes from the push and pull of gravity, the boarder's body fighting the curve of the slope, the energy expelled through the legs, the powder flying—but up in the air, there is none of that. Because clouds are just water vapor, there is no "push" and the only gravity at work is the "pull" on the rider on his harness, dangling at the end of the line like a dead weight.

Further complicating things, the dynamics of the helicopter and the force of the wind at high speed flung Wildman around like a rag doll, and the cold, harsh air made it nearly impossible for him to even pretend that he was gliding with any grace. Adding to that, the clouds up close don't look anything like powdered snow because we were too close to actually see the shape of them, and by the time we were in position, everything was just a mushy soup. It took us several months and a host of contraptions to align the rope in the right way and build a harness that Wildman could use to create snowboard-like movements. Even then, it was a far cry from what we envisioned and, in the end, the final video was a creative disappointment for all of us.

Sure, we had some cool helicopter shots and a great soundtrack, but the overall aesthetic and "wow factor" fell far short of what we had dreamed up. At this point, we were well out of money and, frankly, out of ideas for how to make it better. We resigned ourselves to failure, preparing for the video to launch with a wet thud.

But then something happened.

The day the video dropped, several journalists reached out to us, asking questions about the video. Later that same day, a Gizmodo article popped up, with an enticing headline: "Snowboarding in the clouds is so much cooler than regular snowboarding."

Then the avalanche started. A Dailymotion piece titled "He's snowboarding in the clouds!" was followed by a Bleacher Report article that said, "Adrian Wildman Cenni Snowboards Through the Clouds Attached to a Helicopter." The articles just kept on coming, and the topic gained more and more steam on the internet — which led to the biggest surprise the next morning, when I got a call from a friend.

"Tim, turn on the TV!"

There it was: "Snowboarding In The Clouds" featured on *Good Morning America*! We've had numerous videos that have rocketed to hundreds of millions of views, but this was the first time we'd ever been featured on *GMA*.

After the celebrating died down, the entire experience reminded us of the most important lesson — good things happen when you simply crush the headline.

3. Focus on Curb Appeal

Curb appeal is closely connected to the "Get It" Factor, but more tactical in nature. It refers to how your audience views your overall presence as they're scrolling through their social media.

Much has been written and blogged about concerning what goes into an ideal online headline — which phrases work best, how many words to use, and whether you should include numbers. If you haven't read these articles, it's worth your time to Google "how to create a good video headline," and spend some time learning what's worked for other people, to see if it might work for you. These guidelines can certainly be helpful, but the fact is, they are a set of principles and guidelines that are flexible and ever evolving.

A better way to approach this is to think about your headline and all that it entails (text, image, first few seconds of video, the feeling you want to convey) as the curb appeal of the house you're trying to sell. Any realtor or home flipper knows that fixing up the front of the house, adding some colorful landscaping or painting the door an eye-popping color, can make the difference between a competitive and quick sale and a house that sits on the market for months, without being noticed.

Think of your opening elements the same way. Your text is the description of the place. "Charming gem in heart of downtown," for example. Your thumbnail is the impression from the curb, the freshly painted shutters, the red door, the well-manicured flowerbeds. Your first 3 to 7 seconds are what happens when you open the door, the open-living concept, the sweeping entryway staircase, or whatever enticing and inviting feature your home may have to offer.

All of these components comprise your curb appeal in much the same way that your headline goes well beyond the title or descriptive text of your video. It's a far more holistic approach.

You also need to make sure that all these things play well together. You can't have a front-door color that clashes with the color of your yard, or a kitchen painted vanilla with white-on-white appliances when your front door was promising a blue color scheme with stainless steel appliances. All the parts need to mesh so that they're telling a single cohesive story.

When we go crafting these headlines, we take a very tactical approach. We first focus on the purity of the concept, then match the other assets to the video we are creating. The text, thumbnail, and first 7 seconds must all reflect the key element of the video and resonate with the audience, who ultimately determines whether that idea is worthy of a look and a share.

Sometimes this is a very straightforward exercise.

Take for example our Spider-Man video. Although "Peter Parkour" was the journalistic angle, the YouTube headline needed to be far more tactical and direct. Our actual title for the video was "The Amazing Spider-Man Parkour." (We likely would have titled it simply "Spider-Man Parkour" but "Amazing" was in the title of the film and Sony wanted us to include that.) The thumbnail for the video was an image of Spider-Man in the middle of an impressive parkour flip. The text exclaimed, "How does Spider-Man get around when he runs out of webs? Parkour!" The first 5 seconds of the video show Spider-Man executing a perfect parkour dive-roll over a brick wall. If you were surfing the web and ran into our video, you would know exactly what it is. And if you were a parkour fan, the curb appeal would be very high and would likely draw you in, especially if you also have an interest in Spider-Man.

But with other videos, we needed to be more provocative.

This was especially true when we worked with Prince Ea on his global hit about the public school system. Topics like school education can come off as boring to someone who is randomly searching the web, so for this video to pop we needed a title that really grabbed people. And Prince Ea delivered a brilliant one — "I Just Sued the School System!!!" With a headline like that, how can you not pay attention! *

---

* "I Just Sued the School System!!!" published on YouTube September 26, 2016, from Prince Ea.

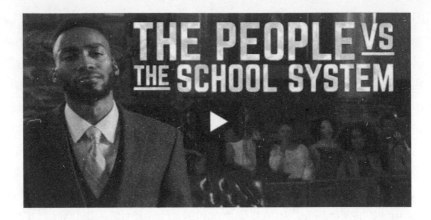

The statement incites intrigue and invites you to find out why he is taking such a bold action. The headline was paired with a thumbnail of Prince Ea in a suit, looking very much like a lawyer in a courtroom. The graphic copy read like it was straight off the legal docket: "The People vs. the School System." And the opening scene was Prince Ea, standing in front of a judge and delivering his opening argument. All these elements combined for world-class curb appeal and, when paired with a unique and engaging video, resulted in one of the most successful PSAs in the history of the internet.

If you're going to go bold, just remember that there is a true difference between being provocative and being insensitive. One example that I always remember because it didn't work was the headline "One-Armed Man Applauds the Kindness of Strangers." Nothing will send people to the exit — or the swipe bar — faster than cringe-worthy, insensitive wordplay. There may be an inspirational story in there, but with this headline, most people won't bother to look. Instead, they question the thoughtfulness of whoever posted it and move on — and that's if they even take the time to understand it.

You also need to be realistic in your headlines. "How to Make a Million Dollars a Day" is a great headline, if you can deliver on it. But since it's so outrageous, it sounds like a charlatan peddling the latest get-rich-quick scheme. If that person does have a formula for making people lots of money, they need to be more specific — and a lot more more believable.

So now that you understand the pieces of curb appeal, make sure that they all work together in harmony. Even we have been guilty of breaking this rule. Going back to our video about snowboarding in the clouds, we nailed the straightforward headline, which was simply "Snowboarding In The Clouds." We had an amazing thumbnail, which was a stunning image of a snowboarder gliding amid a cloud-filled sky. Together, these made for a value proposition that was crystal-clear, and the click rate on the video was extremely high because of it.

But that's where things went wrong.

In the beginning of the video, it took us a whopping 25 seconds before we reached the part where we actually see Wildman snowboarding in the sky. Before then, we show him walking up the mountain and being picked up by a helicopter. In other words, our beginning looks like the beginning of hundreds of other snowboard videos and doesn't deliver on the headline's promise of snowboarding in the clouds. So although we interested people with a compelling headline, and then hooked them with a stunning visual, once they began watching, we didn't deliver on what we had promised. And because we didn't deliver, our curb appeal took a hit. The video still did well, but there's no doubt in my mind that this delay in getting to the action caused us to lose millions of viewers who left the video in the first 10–15 seconds.

4. Give Up the Goat

The term "give up the goat" has multiple meanings (both slang and biblical), but when we use it at Shareability, we are referring to something very specific. To us, giving up the goat means *to give away the best part of the video in the first 7 seconds.*

This is a completely counterintuitive mindset. Traditional storytelling teaches you to build slowly to a climax that happens at the end of the second act. In a feature film, you would never give away how the story ends in the opening credits. It makes no sense, and you'd have an angry audience. But the internet is the complete opposite. With online content, if you don't give people a big payoff in the first few seconds, they are off to the next thing and will never watch the rest of your video. You have to "give up the goat" up front. In the snowboarding video, we should have started by immediately sending Wildman up into the clouds to hook people in right away.

We've found that this strategy is basically guaranteed to put us at odds with any new client. They have been trained through years of traditional advertising to do things in a certain way and are often not accustomed to the rhythm of the internet. A perfect example of this is, well, any surprise-based hidden-camera video we've ever made. I can virtually guarantee that if we are working with a new client who is not accustomed to our standards and practices, and we are creating a surprise video for them, it doesn't matter how many times we tell them that the video *will* start with a tease opening that gives away the entire premise — they will *still* object when they see the first cut.

"You cannot have John Cena pop out of the wall at the beginning of the video! That's supposed to be the surprise that happens later!"

Well, if you don't stick that surprise at the top, no one will be there to see it by the time it happens.

This argument comes to a peak in hidden-camera-surprise videos because the objection feels so logical. It's so ingrained in our storytelling sensibilities that if we are crafting a surprise, we can't reveal it up front. It's like telling a joke by delivering the punch line first. It just doesn't make any sense.

But in digital marketing, it makes all the sense in the world.

One way to think about it—which makes it more palpable to many—is to consider the opening tease as a mini-trailer for the video you are about to watch. It's a quick sugar hit, an instant rush of emotion to make the brain focus and snap into what you're showing before the rest of the story unfolds.

In reality television this is already common practice. Reality shows have been doing this for years, often in the form of what's known as a Super Tease. This is the 2–4 minute trailer for the show that plays at the beginning and shows you exactly what drama and intrigue you are in for over the next hour. Some cooking shows have taken this to extremes and made the opening tease the entire first act. Others have gone even further and actually crafted entire episodes out of this concept, so-called pre-episodes or casting specials, in which they showcase the process of reaching the starting line of the actual show over several hours of television, all cut and crafted as a massive tease for the actual show.

For us and our online work, this tease usually lasts 3–15 seconds. It's the hook that entices people to stick around to see how things will play out. It's the video part of the headline exercise.

Putting the big reveal first sounds backward, but it's part of our contract with the audience, our way of telling them, "Stick around. This is worth your time." You are acknowledging up front that they are going to click on the video, see that it's a full 3 minutes long, and mumble to themselves that they don't really want to watch for 3 minutes. But by putting the visual narrative in the headline—the killer image first—we are telling the audience that this video is going to be worth their while and that they should watch it.

For surprise videos, this is simple—play the best moments from your big surprise and then rewind back into a setup to explain what's going on. For other categories it can be more challenging. It can take the form of a provocative question on screen, a statement that encapsulates the thematic of the piece you are about to watch and makes it seem intriguing, makes the audience lean in and want more.

In other words, you have to give up the goat.

Rule 6

Ride the Wave

Selfie sticks used to be all the rage. Whether at the beach, the amusement park, or the mall, these narcissistic extension poles were everywhere, and they were getting longer. For much of 2015, there seemed to be an unofficial competition online to post the most ridiculous selfie-stick selfie, using the longest, most obnoxious arm.

The extending arm with a phone attached was also turning selfie sticks into a major nuisance. You'd be walking down the street, and everywhere you look, there'd be another pack of nylon-belt-bag tourists posing for a picture, their ring leader in the middle, holding a selfie stick that extended several feet in front of his face, swinging it side to side, making everyone smile so he could pull the trigger.

Things grew so out of control that Disney World officially banned selfie sticks out of safety concerns, after one park-goer tangled up his selfie stick in the car of a roller coaster, causing the ride to be shut down for an hour. Park officials declared that the long selfie sticks were a safety hazard to park-goers, especially to excited children who were running around and not looking out for them.

And the media loved every second of it. It seemed like every day there was a new story about the longest selfie stick or the latest corporate ban. Selfie-stick memes and jokes flooded the internet and became part of pop-culture conversation.

During this time, Pizza Hut approached us to produce a video promoting their new 2-foot-long pizza. In hindsight, you can clearly see where this was going. As had become our normal process, we looked not only to the brand brief (the document that outlines the company's goals for the project) for inspiration, but also to the internet. It didn't take us long to connect the dots. An entertaining video based on the selfie-stick phenomenon was sure to be covered by major bloggers and online media outlets, and would be highly shared.

This is what we call "riding the wave." When you ride the wave, you catch the momentum of a pop-culture topic, put your own spin on it, and, most important, add new value to the topic in some way.

One of the basic principles of shareability and breaking through the internet noise is that it is much easier to attach yourself to something that already has heat than to try to create that heat from scratch. Inserting your brand into trending topics can be one of the most effective ways to attract massive attention, but it can also backfire in a major way, so you have to be very calculated in your strategy.

For Pizza Hut, we decided to reverse-engineer a campaign that would play right into this trend. We knew that the trend itself would lend us shareability, but how could we add value to the conversation? We needed to provide some pop-culture commentary. We needed to have a point of view.

Did we love selfie sticks, or did we hate them? Were they fun, or a public nuisance?

Think about how either of those positions would be received by the public. If you love selfie sticks, and a brand comes out with a video that mocks them, your inner troll would rise up, and armies of annoyed selfie lovers would take to crushing the video in the comments.

On the other hand, what if you hate selfie sticks, and a brand comes out and tells you how much fun they are? You would eagerly dismiss that brand and call them out for callously riding the wave of a trending topic without a clue about what's actually going on.

This is the danger of riding a wave. You can quickly crash and burn. The bigger the wave, the harder the fall. You need to find a perfect line and maintain your balance.

For us, we went through a rapid development phase where we created anything from fake documentary ideas to scripted comedy sketches, all while trying to find the right balance. At some far point, we were even thinking about crafting a fake-news story around homeless people using selfie sticks, to show just how far the trend had gone — it's been said that there is no bad idea in development — but let's just say we recognized pretty quickly that we were barking up the wrong tree!

Where we landed was a perfect sweet spot — we decided *not* to focus on the love or hate relationship with the selfie stick, but rather to focus on the underlying theme, the actual *selfie*. We felt that it was perfectly safe for Pizza Hut to *love* selfies. And if you love selfies, it's not a very big leap to understand that selfie sticks are both an allure *and* a danger. We love selfies and selfie sticks, but if people keep making them longer and longer, the world will no longer be safe. Consequently, we may not be allowed to have them, and that poses a danger to the coveted selfie itself!

We felt that this approach was a comedic and circular argument that played to both sides, and it lent itself very naturally to a specific type of delivery, a mock public service announcement that hilariously presented the dangers of selfie-stick abuse. We cast a likable actress to play the role of a concerned mother, narrating from a gallery littered with selfies, explaining the glories of selfie culture and how these "Vainglorious Van Goghs" were being threatened by the selfie stick.

The video showed selfie-stick users in all kinds of ridiculous situations, from taking selfies in a bathroom stall to a cluster of people struggling to enter an elevator with their sticks at full extension, and a weightlifter extending one off the end of a barbell to capture his biceps at their most flattering angle.

My favorite was the convertible VW Bug with 10-foot selfie sticks poking out everywhere, whizzing through a neighborhood and wiping out a lemonade stand.

In the midst of all the madness, a Pizza Hut delivery man came on to talk about how bigger selfies led to bigger parties, which led to bigger pizzas. "This had better show up on Instagram," he says.

Until the end, when Pizza Hut's logo came up over the final shot of the video, this very subtle integration was the only clue that the video was brought to you by a brand. It was all just pure entertainment, with zero hard sell. Even the end tag was delivered in line with the humor. As the logo comes on, our narrator calmly says: "Pizza Hut is a supporter of those suffering from selfie-stick abuse. Please selfie responsibly."

The campaign was viral gold, rocketing up the YouTube charts and becoming the most shared ad in the world that month, while generating hundreds of articles and widespread media coverage. Sure, the video was funny, but the reason it connected so well was because we found a line that both sides could laugh at, and we added something new to the conversation.

Deciding Which Wave to Ride

I live in Manhattan Beach, California, just a few blocks from the ocean. One of my favorite things to do is to go down to the beach right before sunset and sit in the sand, watching the waves roll in. There are a couple of surfing spots nearby, and I'll often watch surfers as they head into the Pacific Ocean. I've noticed that these surfers have a few different methods of analyzing the ocean and choosing their waves. The most eager surfers hit the water straightaway, paddle straight out, and catch the first wave they can. Others will take a more patient approach, sitting in the surf to gauge the frequency and pattern of the waves, waiting for the biggest one they can find. Still others will stand on the beach and study the waves to see if they want to even bother going out at all. And then there are those who will sit at home and wait for one of their buddies to text them when the waves are going off.

In a similar manner, picking which wave to ride on the internet is analogous to how these surfers choose their waves. You can be proactive and do the work yourself, or you can let others do it for you. At Shareability, we use fairly sophisticated social listening tools to scan and document what people are talking about online. These tools scrape all the major social platforms, like Facebook, Twitter, and Instagram, singling out words and phrases that are being used frequently or paired together, for example. If all of a sudden there is a spike in a certain word or phrase, the listening tool alerts us to the rise in people using that phrase, prompting our social intelligence team to dive deeper. These tools are extremely effective, but they are also expensive. If you don't have the resources to use them, there are much scrappier ways to identify trends and stay on top of digital culture.

The most up-to-the-minute platform, and the easiest one to monitor for the here-and-now of the internet, is Twitter. It has been used to great effect to ride the wave.

While Twitter receives a lot of flak for being an angry place full of bots and trolls, it's also the heartbeat of the internet in many ways. It's the most up-to-date and fastest-moving spot to monitor what's happening in pop culture, breaking news, celebrity gossip, or the latest videos exploding across the web. Twitter is the place that brings it all together.

Generally, trending topics on Twitter end up as hashtags. These are easy to find, but the problem with hashtags is that unless it is something very broad, there can be thousands of active hashtags at a time. A better way to identify trending topics on Twitter is to use the "moments" tab. Clicking on the moments tab shows you what people are talking about on Twitter right now. Much of this content is news related, but it also picks up online-only trends that won't make it to CNN or your local newscast.

We use Twitter to diffuse our content at times as well, but it's primarily useful to us as a social listening tool. In order to use the platform to communicate with your customers, you need time to dedicate to real, one-on-one conversations. This is an amazing opportunity for a brand to talk to its consumers, and some brands are absolutely crushing the platform. But this is not something we typically do for our clients at Shareability, as most already have very capable social media teams running their day-to-day. For us, Twitter is more of a source of inspiration and a place to keep an eye on trends.

If Twitter is the heartbeat of the internet, Reddit is the nervous system. We refer to it as "the place the internet is born." If there is a trending topic or a subject that's starting to boil to the surface, odds are high that it originated on Reddit.

The platform operates like a massive bulletin board. It aggregates social news content, rates web content, and allows people to discuss that content. Posts can be sorted by subjects into user boards called "subreddits," allowing you to narrow a search to your specific interest. The subreddits include endless topics from movies and music to food to animals or super-narrow and niched specifics like memes around one specific celebrity's nose, for example.

Reddit is also very easy to use. Anyone can sign up for free as a "redditor" and submit content to the site. The top of the homepage has tabs allowing you to select from the categories "Hot,"

"New," "Controversial," and "Rising." Another tab allows you to narrow your selection geographically, by state and by country.

That's all well and good, but take a step back and put on your marketing hat. You are now on a platform that is all about user-generated opinions and commentary, where the active population gives an up-or-down vote to each and every single post. Can you imagine a brand trying to shoehorn a commercial into this space? It would be shot down in a nanosecond.

This is why people often say that "Reddit is impossible to crack." But this is a misconception. It's based on the idea that in order to market, you have to somehow "crack" or "hack" or "break" a system, to force it to do something it doesn't want to do. Well, if that's your approach, you haven't been paying attention.

Reddit is just like the rest of the internet—in order to make it work for you, you just need to feed it what it wants. For example, the John Cena meme that we brought to life in our "Unexpected John Cena" video originated on Reddit. When we launched the video, the creator of the original subreddit reacted to the video we made with one of the highest compliments we've ever received: "Wrap it up, boys. We're done for."

That's validation that you not only grabbed the right wave, but that the other surfers in the water appreciated the line you chose and how you executed your ride.

If Reddit is the nervous system, BuzzFeed is your brain reading a gossip magazine. As a publisher, BuzzFeed reports on trending topics, much like a traditional newspaper. True, it may be more along the line of *People* than the *Washington Post,* but still. Correspondents working for BuzzFeed file posts and videos on buzzing topics that often veer closer to water-cooler conversations than hard news. While the site originally focused on viral content, it has since broadened to include traditional news stories across a wide spectrum of topics, and some of their best-performing videos are actually quite meaningful pieces on topics that concern humanity as a whole, from organic farming to restoring coral reefs. While people like to talk about BuzzFeed as a trending topic machine, our viewpoint is that once a story makes it to BuzzFeed, it's often too late to catch that wave. Unless you have something very different to add to the conversation underway, that trend train has already left the station, and you probably need not bother chasing it.

Catching the Wave

So once you've identified a wave, how do you ride it? The first key factor is *speed*. You've been sitting in the sand, watching for the perfect swell, and when it finally comes, it's not gonna slow down to pick you up. You have to be quick. Though the waves on the internet don't disappear as fast as those crashing on Manhattan Beach, you need to catch that wave *before* it crests. All of these waves have fast-approaching expiration dates. If you don't move quickly as a brand or as a personality, you risk losing clout as being internet-friendly, making it seem as though your strategy is being run by a committee that endlessly dithers over what to do.

Probably the fastest we've ever moved to catch a wave was in 2014. It started when we saw an adorable red-headed boy with a pudgy face from Wilkes-Barre, Pennsylvania, named Noah Ritter, who had become an overnight sensation in the way that only the internet can make happen. A local news reporter at the Wayne County Fair was interviewing kids about their experiences on the rides, and she put her microphone in front of Noah, who absolutely stole the show.

"What did you think about the ride?" the reporter asks.

"It was great! And apparently . . . I've never been on live television before. But apparently sometimes I don't watch the news because

I'm a kid and apparently every time apparently grandpa just gives me the remote I have to just watch the Powerball."

It was a completely adorable stream of consciousness, breaking the fourth wall by talking about the interview itself, punctuating every third thought with the word "apparently" and generally just being awesome.

And then Noah literally took the microphone. He began walking around, orating like a pro, going into detail on the ride, and using the word "apparently" the way most teenagers abuse the word "like."

The internet gobbled up the video and dubbed him "The Apparently Kid." The video exploded across the web, racking up more than 30 million views. *

At the time, we were readying our first video for Freshpet and were knee-deep in developing creative concepts. But once we saw

---

* "Apparently Kid's First Ever TV Commercial" published on YouTube September 12, 2014, from Freshpet.

Noah sweeping across the web, we were hooked. And then a light bulb went on — what if we could get "The Apparently Kid" and pair him with adorable puppies? It seemed like an instant hit.

We pitched the concept to Freshpet, and to their credit they quickly embraced it. Green light. Now we just had to make it happen.

The thing that people may not realize is that when someone like Noah goes viral, their life instantly becomes a raging hurricane. Thousands of people are suddenly calling the home phone or reaching out on Twitter or by email, be they journalists, brands, or just adoring fans. It can be quite overwhelming. In Noah's case, the person at the eye of the hurricane was his Grandpa Jack. Jack is Noah's best buddy and protector, and now Jack was the gatekeeper for booking Noah for media requests or brand deals. Things became so crazy so fast that Jack simply turned off his phone. So we were greenlit for a video that we knew would crush, but we couldn't reach the talent. And the clock was ticking. If we didn't put something out into the market extremely quickly, the internet would move on to the next pop-culture darling.

Fortunately for us, my business partner Nick Reed is a former agent and a relentless force when he needs to be. After two days of tracking down Jack around the clock, he finally connected. When Jack found out that Nick was a former military man, we were in! Jack committed to take our deal over all the others that were being offered.

The timing was crazy. It was a Thursday afternoon, and Noah was slated to do an interview with Ellen DeGeneres the following Thursday. Normally with our campaigns, it is a four-to-eight-week process to generate the finished product. But in this case, we had to script the video, have Freshpet sign off, fly Noah to LA, shoot the video, and then edit it all in one week.

We wrote the spot to play into Noah's character from the fair and ride the wave of his popularity. And we also set it up so that Noah could just be Noah, as we knew that the best stuff would be unscripted.

"Today we will be talking about pets," Noah starts on the spot. "Apparently, it's my first-ever TV commercial." He then talks, in his charmingly disjointed way, about the friendship between two dogs named Barney and Ed. The dogs lick his face as he talks about the food. "He didn't like any of the food, and it made his farts stink every day and night."

He continues in his quirky, childlike cadence, talking about how you will have to train your dogs and teach them to play fetch. Then, he brings out a huge plate of dog food for one of the dogs. "Apparently, Freshpet food is the best food than ordinary dog food—he wants to eat it every night and every day." He continues to clown around and go off on charming non sequiturs. As one of the dogs wolfs down the food, he says, "Apparently, that's some good food!"

We filmed and cut the video in time to take advantage of Noah's appearance on *Ellen*. To capture the full wave, we dropped the Freshpet video the morning after the *Ellen* segment aired, as we knew his appearance on the show would generate plenty of buzz. The video rocketed to number two on YouTube globally.

Apparently, as Noah would say, we timed that wave just right.

You can also anticipate seasonal waves. Every year in December, the world is bombarded with holiday-themed advertising, but there are also less obvious seasons and specific days that are recognized throughout the year, from April Fool's Day to International Talk Like a Pirate Day to National Hamburger Day. Every one of these can offer up a wave to ride, provided you time your pop-culture conversation just right.

We did that in 2016 when we developed the Mother's Day campaign around photobombing, just as people jumping in to "bomb" the back of someone else's photo had picked up steam as a pop-culture topic. We took these two seemingly disparate ideas and combined them, turning "photobombing" and "mom" into "PhotoMombing."

The concept sold itself on the headline alone. The idea was that moms were eager to ingratiate their way into their kids' lives, and because their kids were all obsessed with their phones and taking pictures of every single moment of their lives, moms would simply photobomb themselves into every last selfie.

PhotoMombing: Because Moms Are the Bomb

We pitched the idea to a prospective client who we thought the video was perfect for, but they didn't bite. We pitched it to another, and then another, but found no takers. We couldn't understand what was wrong. We *knew* we had a hit on our hands, but nobody seemed to understand it — until this small telecom company we had just started talking to lit up and jumped all over it. Cricket Wireless got it, and that was the beginning of our multi-year partnership with them.

The video paid homage to moms, but did so in an entertaining and amusing way that teenage kids would also enjoy and, more important, would share. The delivery came through a group of mothers on a mission. "Who do you think pays for those unlimited data plans, you little snot monsters," one says, declaring it's time for moms to act. "That's why I am going to photo-bomb the *f . . . un* out of every single selfie." After PhotoMombing their way through their kids' soccer games and parties, the moms all come together to declare: "Talk to your mom. It's Mother's Day, for Cricket's sake!"

The video struck a chord with moms and kids alike, went on to accumulate over 10 million views, and increased Cricket Wireless's Facebook engagement by more than a factor of ten in one month.

Don't Be a Kook

If you've never heard the word "kook," please understand that it is a derogatory surfing term about a beginner with an exaggerated perception of their surfing skills, often coupled with a lack of surfing ethics, which leads them to interfere with the other surfers and their fun in the water. In other words, kooks ruin it for everyone.

In terms of social media, there have been many brands that have accidentally played the role of kook by trying to ride a pop-culture wave without thinking things through. Most of the time this happens when brands try to ride a wave by latching on to a movement to create the illusion that they truly care about a cause, but then fail to actually care in any real or significant way. In short, you have to be authentic when you ride the wave, or you will get busted.

As a result, the shores of the internet are littered with PR wreckage. In 2018, several brands tried to latch on to International Women's Day. The scrutiny was extra high because the #MeToo movement was in full swing, with women telling their stories of being sexually harassed, berated at work, or treated as less than men. Many big brands were eager to come out in support of women on their day, which is a wonderful thing if done *authentically,* but a few of them missed by a spectacularly wide margin.

Among them, there was McDonald's. The fast-food company decided to flip its iconic golden arches upside-down at a restaurant in Lynwood, California, making the "M" a "W" in supposed honor of International Women's Day. It also flipped the "M" on uniforms and packaging at a hundred restaurants. To bring attention to the campaign, McDonald's announced on social media, "Today, we flip our Golden Arches to celebrate the women who have chosen McDonald's to be a part of their story, like the Williams family. In the

U.S., we're proud to share that 6 out of 10 restaurant managers are women."

This all sounds great in theory, but the trouble was that McDonald's wasn't being genuine. The backlash was swift and immediate as critics jumped on the fact that McDonald's was one of the biggest offenders concerning policies and practices that support women workers. Notably, the company has long battled against increasing the minimum wage, which unjustly affects women more than men.

The company was subsequently blasted on Twitter. "Glad to see McDonald's ended sexism by changing their logo into a 'W' for women," one person tweeted. Another wrote: "If McDonald's has flipped their arches upside down to make 'W' for International Women's Day 2018, does that mean all of the other days when it's an 'M' celebrate men?" The executive director of the Democratic Coalition, Nathan Lerner, called them out by tweeting: "Hey @McDonalds, maybe instead of a cheap PR stunt where you make the M a W to 'support' women, you do something real — like pay your workers a living wage."

McDonald's unexpectedly had to spend several days on the defensive. A spokesperson tried to clarify the situation by passing the blame on to its franchisees, saying that more than 90 percent of the chain's restaurants are independently owned and operated, and that those owners set their own policies, wages, and benefits.

But that wasn't the end of it. The backlash against McDonald's gave rise to a new wave for companies to support women in the workplace. In Britain, the activist group Momentum released a video highlighting how low wages and zero-hours contracts at McDonald's meant some women workers faced poverty and even homelessness.

If McDonald's had managed to somehow ride the wave in an authentic and genuine way, they could have benefited. For example, if they took the opportunity to announce that on International Women's Day they were flipping the "M" to a "W" to announce a global initiative to bring real salary parity to the company, or a goal to bring more women into its management ranks, the reception would have been one of cheer rather than scorn and ridicule. Instead, they rushed to catch the wave and were not authentic with the message they tried to ride on, and as a result, they wiped out hard.*

In Malaysia, Kentucky Fried Chicken also made an attempt to ride the wave by changing the image of Colonel Sanders to that of Claudia Sanders, the founder's second wife. A representative of KFC's marketing agency said that KFC was looking for a way to support International Women's Day and found the story of Claudia Sanders, the supportive wife of Colonel Sanders.

But unfortunately, that's where their research stopped. The internet, always at the ready, quickly dug a little deeper and found that the full story, memorialized in book form by Colonel Sanders's daughter, Margaret, was that Claudia was hired by her father to help his first wife with housework and to satisfy his "libido, which required a healthy, willing partner." Oops.†

From disingenuous and lazy, we then go back in time to flat-out tone deaf and downright moronic. The worst attempt in recent memory to ride this wave comes from the frozen-pizza company Di-Giorno. In 2014, there was a movement for women to talk about why

---

* Natasha Bach, "Why McDonald's International Women's Day Celebration Isn't Going as Planned," Fortune.com, March 8, 2018. http://fortune.com/2018/03/08/mcdonalds-international-womens-day-inverted-arches-backlash/.

† Erin DeJesus, "Food Brands Celebrate International Women's Day in All the Wrong Ways," Eater.com, March 8, 2018. https://eater.com/2018/3/8/17096872/food-brands-celebrate-international-womens-day-in-all-the-wrong-ways.

they had remained in abusive relationships under #WhyIStayed. Di-Giorno tweeted out: "#WhyIStayed You Had Pizza." Really?*

Whatever you do — don't be a kook.

Hang Ten

Hanging ten is a very difficult surfing maneuver where the rider steps to the very front, riding with all ten toes poking over the nose of the board. The analogy here is that you must ride with style. You need to add a flourish and help contribute to the conversation. You need to use your own unique voice to add value.

Consider "Fuck Jerry," which is one of the biggest meme sites on the internet. When memes first started going crazy, a creative fellow named Elliot Tebele came up with a simple idea to ride the wave and give it a new spin. In 2013, he launched a tumblr account and started aggregating memes that others had created, sharing them on various platforms. He gave his site an edgy name, a snarky counter-culture reference to *Seinfeld,* and the site quickly became a clearinghouse for memes and a place to generally amuse yourself with hijinks found on the internet.

Even though you could argue that the meat and potatoes of this enterprise is largely to collect and repackage the work of others, the way that it's all wrapped up and repackaged makes the concept unique enough to be a hit. In its success, Elliot's site has also become more and more original over time. By catching the meme wave early and riding it in a unique way, Tebele has created a small media

---

* David Griner, "DiGiorno Is Really, Really Sorry About Its Tweet Accidentally Making Light of Domestic Violence," Adweek.com, September 9, 2014. https://adweek.com/creativity/digiorno-really-really-sorry-about-its-tweet-accidentally-making-light-domestic-violence-159998/.

empire. His followers have crested 14 million, and he's earning serious money. He sells a party game for adults called "What Do You Meme?," he runs a consulting and production studio called Jerry's World, he sells T-shirts and merchandise, and he even has his own brand of tequila.

What's the Bottom Line with Riding Waves?

In sum, if you are trying to push a message out to the world and you are not riding the wave, your odds might be 1 in 2 million. But if you *can* ride a wave, and do it authentically, your odds jump up immediately to 1 in 2,000. Riding the wave dramatically levels the playing field. It's all about how you tie in to a trending topic so that people will be more likely to click on and interact with your content, rather than reject you for being an opportunistic boor. If done right, it's also an effective way to tap into a new audience that you haven't yet engaged with.

But what if everyone is riding the same wave and doing it well? What if the wave is such low-hanging fruit that it looks like the world surfing championships, where everyone is on their game, catching the wave, being authentic about it, and adding value? What if it feels so crowded that even your best material won't be noticed?

Don't fret. There's yet another path to take. That's what the next chapter is about.

Rule 7

Flip the Script

The counterpoint to "ride the wave" is a principle we call "flip the script," meaning to reverse the standard procedure. That is, to do something unexpected or revolutionary, to take trending topics or commonly accepted views and then flip them to the exact opposite.

Being contrarian can be fun. Who doesn't enjoy watching a monkey wrench being tossed into the tedious, monotonous mainstream? The internet *loves* when this happens — provided that it is clever and gives value in some way. And if it's tinged with humor, all the better.

Smart brands have been flipping the script since the early days of advertising. One of the early examples was the print ad from 1959 for the Volkswagen Beetle, also known as the Bug. In a postwar era when Americans were obsessed with "muscle cars" and "bigger is better," the Beetle ad headline simply read "Think small," accompanied, in the corner, by a tiny image of the car. The ad became so successful in "flipping the script" that *Ad Age* magazine named it the best advertising campaign of the 20th century.

Or consider modern Super Bowl ads, the biggest, baddest, and most expensive TV spots in the world. They are typically loud and overproduced, and meant to catch media and online attention as much as the attention of viewers and consumers. Even today, when Super Bowl ads are often released online a week before the game to make sure they don't drown in all the noise, the successful ones are still endlessly judged by people, written about in the press, re-broadcast on newscasts, and shared and commented on online. For many viewers, much of the fun and experience of the Super Bowl is focused more on seeing the creative ads and the glamorous half-time show, and less on the outcome of the actual football game. This kind of scenario makes the Super Bowl the perfect place to the flip the script, to go against the grain, to buck the trend, and to go small when everyone else is going big.

Minimalist Super Bowl spots have long caught people's attention and been highly effective because they are so contrarian. In 1998, FedEx produced a terrific ad that flipped the script, a commercial that was simply 30 seconds of a color-bar screen, the kind that net-works default to when the TV picture goes out. Then, after about 10 seconds of this "attention grabbing nothingness," a simple message came up on screen: "Next time use FedEx. When it absolutely, posi-tively needs to get there." Genius. Because all the other ads were so loud, what stood out was the opposite, an error screen, with a single statement that cut to the heart of the brand's message.

One of the most recent hilarious examples is what Old Milwaukee beer did for the Super Bowl in 2011. The company created an ad with funnyman Will Ferrell. Using a celebrity is helpful to gain attention, but it has also become commonplace for Super Bowl spots, so on its own, having a comedian doesn't really move the needle. But it was the distinctly clever placement of the Old Milwaukee commercial that drove the narrative on Super Bowl Sunday.

The Super Bowl is known as having the biggest advertising audi-ence in the country, and every year the press buzzes about the ex-travagant cost of purchasing a 30-second commercial in the game, with the current price tag running just north of $5 million. In any event, in 2011, Old Milwaukee bought a Super Bowl spot, but to be aired *only* on the local network of the town of North Platte, Nebraska, population about 23,000.

Not only was airing the ad in one small town a total flip of the Super Bowl script of the national audience, but the ad itself was homey and decidedly lacking in any flashiness. Ferrell, wearing shorts and a T-shirt, is seen hoofing it through a field of waist-high wildflowers, to the sounds of serious orchestral music. When he reaches the camera, he is thrown a can of beer. He catches it, pops the tab, and the beer fizzes. And just as he begins his sales pitch with "Old Milwaukee . . ." he is suddenly cut off, and the ad ends. *

Not surprisingly, the "smallness" of the commercial soon became the subject of major internet chatter. A few people in North Platte, Nebraska, used their phones to record the ad, and then they posted the video online. The ad spread like wildfire once people realized that no other towns in America were seeing the ad. People loved

---

* Old Milwaukee Super Bowl XLVII commercial originally televised February 5, 2012.

the anti–Super Bowl nature of the ad, and because Old Milwaukee was pretending that it didn't want people to see the ad, the internet wanted it even more. Do you think the people recording the ad and posting it online were in any way affiliated with the marketing effort behind it? If that was our campaign, we would have made sure of it.

Even though you aren't likely to be running a Super Bowl ad, even a localized single-town version, there are lessons to be learned from what major brands with seemingly unlimited ad-spending capability have done on the most crowded, noisy day of advertising of the year — flipping the script by taking something that is supposed to be big, and then going small with it. This is the right idea, no matter the trend. If you buck it and come up with a creative way to go in the opposite direction, and you can make sure it fits your brand message, then you too can flip the script and use that momentum to stand out.

Programming a Counter-Narrative

While you could argue that everything we do flips the script on marketing, let's look at a specific example, especially as it pertains to the idea of trends. One of the key components of both riding the wave and flipping the script is to find out what is trending. You can attach yourself to a trending topic to ride the wave, or to flip the script by finding a trending topic to turn it on its head. You are looking to program with — or counter to — the latest conversation or trend.

A few years ago, the concept of pet shaming was trending like crazy. People love their pets, so animal topics tend to gain steam online fairly quickly, particularly when they're funny. Pet shaming was born when people began putting a sign around their pet's neck or next to its bed or food bowl whenever the pet did something bad, and then taking a picture or video of the animal looking sheepish.

The signs said things like "I ate the sofa," "I pooped on my Mom's favorite pillow," or "I ate the baby's shoe." It was sort of like a dunce cap for the animal.

At the time, we had just begun working with Pets Add Life, a committee that advocates for pets and how they enhance people's lives. We've had a lot of success with animal videos and knew how powerful they can be, but we were also aware of the seemingly endless supply of pet videos that already exist across the web. We needed something unique and different to help us break through. As our brain trust was going through the process, they found the trend on pet shaming and realized all we had to do was flip the script — instead of humans shaming pets, what if we had the pets shaming the humans?

Done. Best idea ever. At least on paper.

We went down a million different roads trying to figure out how to crack this seemingly obvious idea. Should we have animals taking pictures of humans in embarrassing situations? How would they do that? Did we need to see them holding the camera? Were the humans aware they were being photographed? Were they asleep? If so, how did the pets re-create the moment?

The concept was great, but what was the actual video?

Eventually, we landed on a winner. We created a campaign called "Attention All Humans!!! | Stop Pet Shaming." * It opens with a dog talking to the camera. Yes, literally talking to the camera. The mouth was animated and the voice, after several attempts by various high-caliber actors, was one of our favorite writers, Dave Ackerman. I don't know if it's the beard or his jovial nature, and I mean this in

---

* "ATTENTION ALL HUMANS!!! | STOP PET SHAMING" published on You-Tube December 12, 2016, from Pets Add Life.

the most loving way possible, but he sounds exactly like what a dog speaking English should sound like.

"Hey, human. Stop scrolling for a second, I gotta talk to you," the dog says, staring into the camera. "You think you are so funny, turning us into an internet meme, putting all of our weakest moments on your phone for the whole world to see. You and your phones . . . And you have the nerve to call us your best friend. How would you like it if the tables were turned?"

The pets then turn the tables, and we see the humans doing things they would *not* want posted on social media and being called out by their pets. While cuddling on the couch and watching TV with her boyfriend, a woman passes gas.

She quickly accuses her dog, who is sleeping at her feet. We pan down next to the dog to a sign that reads: "That was you and you know it." The guy, knowing it was her, wrinkles his nose and looks at the girl, who shakes her head, contining to deny it was her. Cut to the dog's next sign: "Yes it was. You have IBS and it's a problem."

The solution to the complex development questions turned out, as is so often the case, to be super simple. We would just have the pets display the signs that shame the humans. Did they write them? We don't care, we didn't see that part! It was a simple solution that kept the humor of the core idea without overcomplicating any of the execution.

After the video shows a string of pets shaming humans, our dog narrator asks for reconciliation. "Look, we all do some pretty weird things in private," the dog says, adding, "but those moments don't define us. Being your best friend no matter what, that's what we're all about. That's who *we* are." He encourages humans to keep doing those weird things, and suggests, accompanied by images of a guy and his parrot bobbing to hip-hop, that pets might even join in. "Just remember," he says, "we didn't tell anyone about that time you . . . you know."

The video ends with the caption "Skip the shaming. Share this instead. #PetsAddLife." And people did. It received over 5 million views and over 1,000 shares.

Bring Something Different to the Party

Flipping the script works for influencers as well, provided they are bringing something completely different to the table or providing a twist. More than a different point of view, like the conservative-versus-liberal debate in cable news, this requires looking at people who are already thought leaders in your space, to see *how* they are providing their commentary — and then creating something so original and different that it attracts the same audience they have already hooked, by offering them something new and fresh, a complementary counterpoint.

In 2015, YouTube was full of engaging influencers with warm, positive personalities. Everywhere you clicked on YouTube, someone was motivating you, pushing you to be your best self, or waxing positive about their life. The rise of iJustine, a self-proclaimed "lifecaster," and Rosanna Pansino, known for her bubbly baking videos, opened a door for a different, more irreverent voice to emerge.

Enter Poppy. A young lady who looked downright weird, even by the internet's loose standards of weird-dom. She came onto the scene so different, so counterculture, and so understated that it was almost impossible not to pay attention to her. She was the exact opposite of all the vloggers whose brands were all about being likable and spreading sunshine, and even more amazing, she had no message at all. *

* "It's Time" published on YouTube August 20, 2018, from Poppy.

Poppy came about when 15-year-old Moriah Pereira, wanting to break into the entertainment business, moved from Nashville to Los Angeles. Her actual performance talent may have been singing, but like so many others with talent, she wasn't going anywhere until she was noticed. She turned to the internet, studied the influencers whose sites were exploding, and saw what was missing: the *opposite* of what everyone else was doing.

She adopted her nickname Poppy and began making abstract videos that were authentically her. Her director and producer, Titanic Sinclair, described them as a combination of "Andy Warhol's pop accessibility, David Lynch's creepiness and Tim Burton's zany comedic tone." Whether that's an overstatement or not didn't really matter, because people started watching and they didn't stop.

In her first breakout video, "Poppy Eats Cotton Candy," she is dressed in a pink tutu, eating pink cotton candy. That's all that happens for a minute and a half. The colors are muted, the contrast nonexistent; Poppy savors the cotton candy, licks the stick, and smiles at the camera at the end. That's it.

Another big hit took the concept of odd simplicity to a whole new level. In a childish monotone with varying inflections, she repeats "I'm Poppy" for 10 minutes straight. That's right, 10 minutes of "I'm Poppy. I'm Poppy. I'm Poppy . . ."

Both videos have an oddly transfixing quality, but more important, they were so far removed from all the other YouTubers trying to deliver a careful and poignant message to help people with their relationships or to bake muffins. Poppy touched a nerve in young people who were living online, always hunting for the next new thing, because it gave them a reprieve from anxiety, a break from always absorbing information about how to live their lives. Instead, these Poppy videos offered an opportunity to just enjoy something odd for a minute.

Poppy rose to internet fame by flipping the script, an act that also helped her find her voice. The videos gained her some 50 million followers. Using the internet as her stage, her career took off. She signed a record deal with Island Records and embarked on a tour to support her first album. She starred in a series of videos with the spot-on title "Internet Famous with Poppy" for Comedy Central, and even wrote a book titled *The Gospel of Poppy,* which, you guessed it, flips the script on biblical stories by parodying them.

This is a young lady who understands how the internet works, that when a wave becomes too strong in one direction, it's ripe to be disrupted with a 180-degree turnabout. The internet will gladly, and with open arms, embrace something totally the opposite of what's popular, but hitting that nerve requires someone with a unique voice. If anyone has found her voice, it's Poppy.

Playing Against Type

One way to flip the script without having to obsessively monitor trends is by simply taking an established personality or idea, and then turning it against type. It's kind of like putting Robert De Niro in his first comedic role, casting against type. Everyone will pay attention to see if he can nail the part, and if he does, it simply adds another dimension to his career. Safe to say, De Niro has done that.

This was the line of thinking we followed when we set out to launch a headphone company with one of the most famous people in the world: We flipped the script by making him anonymous.

Cristiano Ronaldo is one of the most recognized stars on the planet, known by 86 percent of people in the world, according to *Time.* He has one of the largest social media footprints in the world, with over 250 million followers. He hails from Portugal but lives in

Spain, where he is God-like famous. Every time people saw Ronaldo in an ad for Nike or Calvin Klein, he looked like a movie star: glamorous, glorious, and distant. He was perceived as an untouchable, Adonis-like superstar.

So we decided to take the opposite tack. Instead of simply filming the sharp and polished superstar the way everyone else always had, we turned him into a vagabond. We pasted an ill-groomed beard on him, gave him a bit of bulk under some droopy clothes, and put him in the streets of Madrid, where he tried to make people notice him by doing tricks with a soccer ball. Without a disguise, he wouldn't have lasted five seconds before being mauled by a mob of fans, but because he looked like a down-on-his-luck everyman, nobody cared or paid attention to him.

For over an hour he performed trick after trick, growing more and more desperate to attract people's attention. He kicked the ball to a passerby, who merely tapped it back to him and then scurried away. He playfully asked a woman for her phone number, but was rebuffed. He then dribbled the soccer ball in and around people, upping the ante on his tricks. Midway through his soccer hijinks, he flopped down on the ground in mock exhaustion.

Despite all of his best efforts, Ronaldo in disguise was pretty much ignored. Until finally, a curious little kid showed some interest in his sleight-of-foot act. He returned the ball, and a bit of an interplay between the two unfolded. The bum asked the kid to show him what he could do, and the kid lobbed the ball up and down a few times before returning it. He had some skill! The disheveled man started dribbling, asking him to try and take the ball off him. The kid did it! The man picked the ball up and gave him a high-five, then he asked him to hold on for a second. He started pulling at his beard, pulled it all the way off, and revealed his true self: international superstar Cristiano Ronaldo.

Within a matter of seconds the square was packed. People stopped and flocked around him. Ronaldo barely had time to sign the ball and to give it to the kid before he was rushed off to safety by his security detail, surrounded by a mob of screaming fans who now recognized their hero.

This was a very shareable video because it showed Ronaldo in a way he had never been seen before. It was also counterprogramming to the hero worship of celebrities, allowing one of them to become invisible as an ordinary citizen for a moment. It didn't offer any specific commentary or point of view on the cult of personality. But the mere fact that people were ignoring such a huge star, even though he was in an open public square displaying his immense skills with a ball—the exact thing that is the cause of his fame in the first place—was commentary enough. People were intrigued and drawn in.

Of course, before the video launched and we were showing the rough cut to viewers, everyone told us it was great, but it was just way too long. The video was over 4 minutes. That's an eternity in traditional advertising. It's like eight Super Bowl spots. For much of it, nothing really happens. Ronaldo even looks like he wants to take a nap at one point!

We were unilaterally told by experts in the field that we had to simply edit and cut the video in half. Even 2 minutes was more than the fickle internet could really handle.

Good thing we didn't listen. These 4 minutes launched the global brand ROC. In addition to over 100 million views, more than 2,500 articles were written about the video in 22 languages around the world. The brand became a pop-culture sensation, and we had spent a tiny fraction of the cost of traditional advertising.

For any major brand, this is a virtual template for launching a new product line. And it was done by merely flipping the script.

When the Internet Flips the Script on You

The internet has a mob mentality and loves to disrupt and upset anything that feels like it's from the ruling establishment, especially self-aggrandizing corporate promotion. Flipping the script on a brand's best-laid promotional plans is a constant and favorite activity on social media.

When this happens, brands need to be fast-footed in their response and open to adapt and to change their initial strategy. Their response determines whether they will dig themselves a deeper hole or build a mountain of goodwill. Defensive posturing and pushback are typically met with internet mobs turning the volume up on their negative comments. In other words, the best way for a brand to respond when the internet flips its script is to instantly accept the new reality.

This is a lot like the dictum in improvisational comedy, the "Yes, and" rule that stipulates that you cannot deny, you can only accept and move on. If you are engaging in improv repartee with someone, you must go with the flow of whatever they do or say to keep upping the ante. You cannot deny the reality they've created. Say someone makes the shape of a gun with their hand and says, "Stick 'em up." You can't say, "That's not a gun, that's your finger." That would be tantamount to saying "No," which is not allowed. You must say "Yes" and accept that the hand is now a gun, and then respond to that reality. Brands that have the script flipped on them need to have that same sense of humor — whether they like it or not.

Walmart was put in this position when it launched an online promotion for hip-hop artist Pitbull to perform a free concert in the parking lot of a hometown's Walmart. The contest was sponsored by Sheets Energy Strips, which are Listerine-like breath strips, and the rules were straightforward: Whichever town received the most votes online during the designated time period would win the concert.

The idea was to promote community pride. Everyone was supposed to vote for their town and to tell all their friends on social media to vote, so they would end up with Pitbull jamming at their local Walmart. Did the internet comply? Not a chance! The mob mentality of the internet decided instead to make a joke at Walmart's expense, rallying around some obscure town to drive the show into the middle of nowhere. Mobs love it when you give them an opportunity for power, even over the silliest things.

When the campaign was launched, David Thorpe and Jon Hendren of the website Something Awful mischievously asked people to vote for Kodiak, Alaska, an island town with a population of 6,191. It was the smallest town in America to carry a Walmart. As the prank built steam and Kodiak gained votes in far greater numbers than its population, Walmart was faced with two options: Deny what was happening and scrap the promotion as rigged, or just play along.

Smartly, Walmart rolled with the punches and didn't try to stop the movement. Almost more important, neither did Pitbull. He posted a video with clips of his current world tour, saying he would go anywhere for his fans, and invited the people who came up with the joke to "follow me to Kodiak."

And so, because the internet flipped the script on Walmart, Pitbull flew to Kodiak. After being received in local fashion and gifted with bear repellent, he rocked the Walmart parking lot as advertised. In the end, both Walmart and Pitbull received far more and far *better* attention than they would have if the promotion had simply played out as originally envisioned.

Flipping the script, whether it's by going small when everyone is going big, putting the shoe on the other foot, casting against type, or playing along if the script is flipped on your brand, is the yin to riding the wave's yang. They are two sides of the same coin when it comes to attaching your message to the vox populi, or bucking it altogether. This can be applied to any message you want to put out, even on topics that are not obviously exciting, from community issues, to social good or dentistry. It's a way to take the tedious and make it into the exciting.

Know Your Platforms

Shawn Mendes is a global superstar. He is the first pop artist to have four number-one hits before the age of 20. He headlines tours around the globe and has a whopping 100 million–plus followers on social media. But it wasn't always this way. Mendes didn't go to pop-star university or get discovered after ten years of touring in clubs. He made it by simply creating his own fan base on the internet.

Growing up in Pickering, Ontario, a smallish town outside Toronto, Mendes always knew that he wanted something bigger. So, at the age of 14, he learned to play the guitar and started posting videos on Vine, in which he played 6-second covers of songs by Justin Bieber, Ed Sheeran, and Adele. What Mendes lacked in formal music training he made up tenfold with raw talent, magnetic charm, and an innate understanding of how to connect with people online. He posted new videos religiously and quickly accrued a loyal following, running up 1 million followers on Vine and 400,000 on Twitter — all from his parents' house in Pickering.

This all came naturally to Mendes, who told *Rolling Stone,* "I was one of those kids who was just always on the Internet, always on YouTube, so it was easy for me to do it. It's not work. It's just fun."*

---

* Brittany Spanos, "Shawn Mendes: How a Toronto Teen Became the Super-

That "fun" led Mendes to being discovered on YouTube by talent manager Andrew Gertler, who immediately flew Mendes and his family to New York and put him in the studio. Gertler soon landed Mendes a recording deal with Island Records. Mendes's first single followed shortly thereafter. It rocketed to number one on iTunes and put him on tour with global pop star Taylor Swift and eventually on his own headlining tour.

Mendes's story shows the incredible power of social platforms like YouTube, Twitter, and Instagram to connect with audiences and build a large and passionate fan base outside the traditional Hollywood power structure. These platforms give everybody the chance to share their stories and talents with the world.

In this chapter, we're going to dig deep into the actual platforms to gain a thorough understanding of all of the intricacies and technical details that you need to know to be successful. I want to arm you with the know-how to look at all of the platform options and understand where your type of content might be a good fit, and how it can be specifically tailored to break through.

The stakes are high. There are myriad platforms, and they are changing and evolving every day. What worked yesterday might be a death knell tomorrow, and no matter how sharp your content is, if you don't understand all the different options, your efforts will fail.

Having said that, in the words of *The Hitchhiker's Guide to the Galaxy*'s author Douglas Adams, which legendary sci-fi author Arthur C. Clarke called the best advice that can be given to humanity: "Don't panic."

Several times a year we see real anxiety set in across the brand

---

star Next Door," *Rolling Stone*, April 13, 2016. https://rollingstone.com/music/music-news/shawn-mendes-how-a-toronto-teen-became-the-superstar-next-door-237177/.

community as a report comes out that some platform is changing its algorithm to reposition all their content. "Facebook now limiting status updates, feed reaches fewer followers. Is this going to lead to the death of online video?"

No, it isn't.

People bang their heads against their keyboards in frustration, write angry posts about how Mark Zuckerberg is killing their business, and cry foul about the ever-changing nature of the bourgeoning industry they've chosen to work in. They spend hours and hours and hard-earned money to rejigger their messages — only to receive news a month later that the algorithm is changing yet *again*.

If you believe the tech news, you will constantly feel like you need a team of MIT data scientists to keep up with all the latest platform changes. But I am here to tell you not to panic. Sure, the algorithms will change, and yes, that may affect how your content is viewed or shared in some way. But the fact of the matter is that if you focus on the big-picture concepts that are outlined in this book, you can consistently outperform your competition, no matter what algorithm changes come your way.

This is why I will spend a lot of time, in this chapter and the next, explaining all the different ways in which these platforms affect you and how you can adapt to them in order to maximize your results. The key is to conceptually understand the motivations and incentives that *drive* these platforms, to fundamentally realize what they are built to do, and how they all fit together to form our social ecosystem, so that you can make that system work for you.

A Big-Picture View

Before we dive into the specific platforms, let's take a step back and look at the idea of social networks as a whole. For us, there are three big-picture concepts around the philosophy of social media that are essential to understand.

1. Social networks were built for their users.

This may sound obvious, but it's surprisingly counterintuitive. Most people, even experts in our field, don't understand this.

Look back at traditional networks, both TV and radio. They were built from the ground up to serve one master only: the advertisers. They exist only to offer an audience to brands that want to pay to promote their products on the airwaves they control.

But isn't that also true for all the social media platforms as well? What is Facebook if not a massive audience-gathering mechanism with billions of eyeballs available for a price? The difference is that social platforms weren't necessarily *built* for that purpose. They were created to allow people to connect and share information about their lives. That is their (original) sole reason for being.

I can't tell you how many brand boardrooms I've been in where the executives treat social media platforms as some kind of post-modern advertising delivery system for brands. They talk in terms of "impressions," "paid distribution," and "conversion rate." As if Insta-gram was created just so that they could sell their candy bar to some kid in Indianapolis.

But social networks are a different beast. There, the exploitation of the audience for profit is an add-on, not the essence, as it is in traditional broadcasting. True, it may be crucial, and the source of billions of dollars in revenue, but it's not a core functionality — and this makes all the difference.

Whether you are a brand or a personality, to succeed on these platforms you need to always understand the mindset of the users, as well as the unwritten rules that define the ecosystem. You are effectively an uninvited guest on these platforms — no one is checking their Facebook account to see the latest deal from a wireless carrier — so you had better act accordingly.

This comes back to Rule 3: Focus on value. As a guest on these platforms, you want to be focusing on *providing value* to the viewers instead of taking it. You'll make a lot more friends that way.

My partner, Nick Reed, often tells an anecdote of being at a cocktail party and how to apply social etiquette. If you were talking to friends and a new person stormed up to your group and immediately asked to borrow $20 for cab fare, what would you say? How fast would you run away? Conversely, if that same person approached you and introduced themselves with a handshake and a smile, and you spent the next 30 minutes having a pleasant and lively conversation about life, your kids, and how much you both hate commuting, how much better would that feel? And if after that conversation, that person told you, with a hint of embarrassment, that they had misplaced their wallet and asked if they could borrow $20 for a cab home, would you loan it to them? I bet you would.

That is the same mindset that you should take to social media.

2. Each platform is unique.

While there is a common core to all social platforms, they are also deeply unique, each with its own purpose and modus operandi — a deep focus on a specific problem that it is trying to solve for its users.

They all do it in their own unique language, which is a combination of specifically formatted text, photos, videos, and emojis that guide how people communicate with their friends, family, and followers. Each has its own rhythm and cadence in terms of how often people post, how deep or shallow the content is, and how active or passive the user experience is.

For years, people have been talking about how different YouTube is from traditional television. This is certainly true, but in terms of user experience, Instagram is as different from YouTube as YouTube is from TV, Twitter is as different from Snapchat as WhatsApp is from Facebook. They are all totally and completely different universes, each with its own rules and guidelines. Always keep this in mind as we set out to understand and conquer the various social platforms.

Later in this chapter I will delve into all the major platforms in detail. We'll talk through the ones that we view as being the most valuable for brands, including YouTube, Facebook, and Instagram, as well as a bucket of what we refer to as Direct Messaging Platforms, including Twitter, Snapchat, and Reddit. In my opinion, you can't even begin to succeed on social media until you understand the differences that make each platform unique.

3. One size does not fit all.

This should be obvious by now, but because of the differences among the platforms, you must vary your strategy and execution for each one. That is, you can't throw a YouTube video on Facebook and hope it works because, well, it won't.

In the brand world, a philosophy of "content everywhere" has emerged over the past few years. This usually means that most corporate brands take their commercially heavy-handed videos and spread them across all their social media channels. Of course, since Instagram won't allow a video over 60 seconds, the brand will simply make a shorter version for that platform, but it's still the same video.

This is extremely misguided. Imagine Fox TV partnering with theater chain AMC to launch each episode of *Dancing with the Stars* as a feature film cut-down on 2,000 screens across the United States *and* making it a podcast at the same time. It doesn't make sense. Who wants to go to a movie theater to watch a talent show? Who wants to listen to a dance program? That's not how we consume our entertainment.

In the same way, you can't take a video that was custom-made for Facebook and jam it onto Snapchat, or take an image-heavy strategy for Instagram and think it is going to have any success on YouTube. They're completely different worlds, and they require different tools, styles, and cadences to be effective. And yes, doing this right takes a *lot* of work, but it's the only way to ensure success.

Looking at these three guiding principles, you'll find it becomes obvious that the overhyped concept of "content everywhere" basically translates to "effective nowhere." My recommendation is to always take the complete opposite route: Instead of spreading yourself too thin and trying to master every platform, which will only make you feel overwhelmed with the complexity and exhausted by the constant failure, you should start by diving deep into one platform. Focus on the platform that suits your needs best and create a test-and-learn methodology (which I will outline in the next chapter) that allows you to experiment your way to success and eventually a mastery of your platform of choice.

This is what successful social celebrities like Jay Shetty (Facebook), Furious Pete (YouTube), and Amanda Cerny (Snapchat) have done. Only after you have mastered one platform should you move to the next one. That's how you gradually become a standout. For inspiration, look at what Red Bull has done on YouTube, what Airbnb has created on Instagram, * or how Wendy's has stirred things up

* Airbnb via Instagram.

on Twitter. These are brands that spent the time and resources to master a platform, and they are enjoying the benefits of that success.

Now that we've talked about these platforms in general terms, let's move into the specifics. I've always struggled to come up with an analogy to describe the various social platforms in a clear, easy-to-understand way. Randomly, I was sitting in a meeting the other day when one of our strategists, Patrick Mazuca, started describing the different platforms as different pieces of a city. I thought that was brilliant. Like most analogies, it's not perfect, but I think it goes a long way toward explaining the role that each platform plays in people's online life, in much the same way that each of the buildings or institutions works for a city. So without further ado, here is Patrick's overview of the "city of the internet."

YouTube: The Public Library

If the internet is a city, then YouTube functions as the internet's library. In 2019, when someone goes to YouTube, more often than not, they do so with a very specific intention. This is similar to the mindset of the old days, when people would walk into a library looking to find a book or article on a specific topic. Users today search YouTube for the content they desire, whether that be the latest music video, an explanation on how to change your spark plugs, or some inspiration on what to cook for dinner tonight.

The search element may be a core functionality of YouTube today — they are owned by Google after all — but it's something the platform has grown into over time. Created in 2005 and bought by Google in 2006, YouTube was originally a viral video platform. It was the first major site that allowed people to show themselves off to the world on the internet and to build their personal brands. In a sense, YouTube was created to be television for the internet, with every citizen serving as both broadcaster and audience.

YouTube channels in the early days were — and to a large extent still are — heavily focused on their owners or programmers. There was an expectation that the person who ran the channel would be featured *in* the content, that they would be the star of their show. With few exceptions, influential YouTubers wouldn't post another person's or company's video on their channel.

Early YouTubers were a trigger point in altering the branding landscape. As millennials turned away from television to more original and outrageous content on the internet, a new generation of media stars was born. This period was fueled by a sense of discovery — young people felt like they were uncovering new talent, rather than having it forced on them by out-of-touch media companies, and this created an audience that was far more vested in the talent's success. They felt a sense of *ownership*.

This was a new awakening for the next generation of filmmakers and led to an explosion of video sharing. As the market expanded, the quality of the content increased dramatically. Some videos were shot in super-high 4K resolution and contained cinematic storytelling worthy of feature films, but they all brought a vibe and perspective that was specific to the creator and uniquely millennial.

It wasn't just the quality that was getting better. Over the past ten years the *quantity* of content went from a modest drip to a full-blown global flood. In 2019, more than 500,000 hours of content is uploaded to YouTube *every single day*. Think about that: 500,000 hours. In just one day. That is an astounding statistic and has meant two things for the platform.

First, the overwhelming volume of content has made it nearly impossible for regular people and brands to "go viral" on the platform. Obviously it can still happen, but the odds are so stacked against you that it really should not be a core part of your strategy.

Second, this insane volume of uploaded content has made YouTube the ultimate clearing-house for online videos on basically any topic that you could ever imagine.

This evolution has allowed YouTube to grow into something far more interesting than originally intended. All the content launched on YouTube is *stored* on YouTube, meaning it can be retrieved by interested users. Once YouTube started sorting these billions of hours of content by category, aided by users identifying keywords and phrases in the video, the platform very much became the public library of online video.

Over the past five years, the platform has shed the image of viral immediacy and become known for its long search tail. Because YouTube is owned by Google, the internet's most popular and effective search engine, the search mission is now ingrained in its DNA, and they have pulled this function off with stunning success. In 2018, over 5 *billion* videos were watched on YouTube every single day. To put that in perspective, the average cable television station has around 500,000 viewers in a day. That's not apples to apples, but it gives you an idea of where this world is heading. Because of search, YouTube has become the behemoth in terms of how we consume video content online.

And to ensure it continues to grow, YouTube now pays far more attention to individualizing the experience on the site than to blitzing users with viral content. The site is focused on helping you find specific content using search and on giving you what you want, using their artificial intelligence (AI) algorithm to tap into your preferences or your previous searches.

The AI algorithm is a contentious issue. Proponents claim that AI will know what you want better than you do. But, of course, because we are still in the early days of sophistication, there are also plenty of examples where this goes horribly wrong.

On the positive side, the YouTube library now is smart enough to show most users only what they are truly interested in. If Lisbeth in Pennsylvania loves cooking and has spent hours searching and watching food-related content, the algorithm will happily put new cooking videos in front of her every time she logs on. If she starts searching for a vacation in the Catskills, the algorithm will switch, adding some vacation rentals and travel tips into the mix. This is very similar to going to the library and browsing cookbooks, then moving over to the travel section. You will find what you are looking for because the content is grouped together in a logical way.

The negative spin comes into play when users search for more polarizing, controversial, or weighted topics. If Andy in Montana goes looking for videos about the Holocaust and happens to click on something that spins some tale of denial, the algorithm might happily send him deep into a rabbit hole of conspiracy theory and propaganda that, if taken at face value, will teach him the Holocaust never happened. It will be up to Andy to recognize and realize the fact that these videos are deceptive and to seek out better and more accurate information, as the still immature algorithm can't help him with that.

If Lisbeth uses the wrong kind of pepper, she might have a disappointing meal. If impressionable Andy accepts what he's being presented with as fact, the consequences might be dire.

These are extreme examples, but they are unfortunately all too real. Using YouTube as a search engine for video has become so ingrained in our society that no one goes onto the site to flip through channels at random. People know what they are looking for, and rather than scrolling through hundreds of videos on topics that don't interest them, they watch what they want to watch, regardless of how many views the content may have racked up.

This can have amazingly positive results. My father-in-law, John Frink, is a perfect example of the benefits of YouTube having evolved into the internet's library. Last summer, he wanted to create a garden gnome for our back patio, as a gift. He went on YouTube, something he never would have done five years ago, and typed in "How to make a garden gnome."

Presto, a seemingly endless list of results popped up. He scrolled through and watched the four videos that looked the most interesting. Which ones were those? You guessed it — they were the ones that had the best headlines and thumbnail images that connected to his DIY-related search. One of the videos provided the most value, an easy and straightforward way to build a garden gnome from scratch, complete with step-by-step instructions, from a channel called MontMarteArt. The thumbnail was a freeze frame of someone applying paint to an almost-finished gnome. The title was equally captivating: "Art Lesson: How to Make Your Own Garden Gnome Using Air-Hardening Clay." *

Here, an energetic and engaging host walks you through how to create a garden gnome, step by step, from simple materials that you can buy at your local hardware or home improvement store. The video is 10 minutes long and is the perfect guide for the amateur who is doing this for the first time, wants professional-looking results, and would be completely lost without it. John followed the instructions, rewatched the video dozens of times, and ultimately

---

* "Art Lesson: How to Make Your Own Garden Gnome Using Air-Hardening Clay" published on YouTube November 22, 2012, from MontMarteArt.

built an outstanding garden gnome that has since garnered him lots of comments and praise. *

John's project is a good example of YouTube at its finest. He "went to the library," did his research, and found a video that gave him the information and guidance he needed. Now that the gnome project is complete, the next time John goes to YouTube, his need will be completely different. This is a pretty good way to think about YouTube and how most people use it.

So what does this mean for you?

When you're creating content for YouTube, you need to think about this search functionality from both a philosophical perspective as well as a technical one.

———————————

* Photograph by John Frink.

1. The YouTube Philosophy

In Chapter 3, I wrote at length about focusing on value to create successful content. This is an important concept on any social platform and especially relevant to YouTube. Think about the case of my father-in-law. He wasn't roaming the web, surfing for some cool content or flipping through the channels of YouTube, trying to fill an hour on a lunch break. He was there to find value on a very specific subject matter — how to build a garden gnome.

Tens of millions of people do that very same thing every single day, looking to solve a specific problem. If you're a brand or a personality, think about the type of content that would be valuable to the consumers or audience that you want to reach, then put yourself in their shoes and ask, What type of content would they search for? Then think about what your expertise is and how that crosses over with what they want. What are you uniquely qualified to offer that this audience would find valuable? Figure out what that means for you, and make that.

Let's say you are a home improvement store, such as Home Depot. With a traditional advertising mindset, you would run paid ads across YouTube that attempted to tell the audience how you are the place to go for home improvement. Of course, you would use the sophisticated algorithms to target people who are searching for home improvement videos already, so you are sure to have a captive audience, right?

Wrong. The ads would run in front of and interrupt the content that your audience actually *wants* to watch, so they will most likely skip and tune out your ads whenever they can. What do they care about your glossy, slick commercial if they are here to learn how to repaint their bedroom!

That may sound harsh, but that's just the way things work in the internet age.

Instead, let's say you focus on value instead—what type of content would you create? If you're Home Depot, start by taking a look at your strengths. Not only are you an expert on all things home improvement, but you also have incredibly detailed data on the types of home improvement products that people buy, both online and in your stores. Using that data, you could identify a series of the most popular or necessary home improvement projects and create content specifically designed to create value in those areas. For example, if one of the most common home improvement projects is painting a bedroom, you would create a series of videos that show the viewer the easy-to-follow steps to paint their bedroom with the least amount of time and effort. Or better yet, what if the video showcased how you could paint your room like a professional, but for a fraction of the cost of what you would pay a professional painter? Hey, that might be interesting to the people searching YouTube for "how to paint my bedroom."

Now you're thinking about what the audience actually wants. You can start to produce videos like "How to build the kitchen of your dreams," "How to save money on your water bill," and "How to create a garden that will make your neighbors jealous." The topics are endless.

There are two important dynamics at play here.

Number one, major brands like Home Depot have huge marketing budgets, meaning that they have the resources to make the best content in these types of categories. Sure, there are a lot of experts who could do it, but there are very few who could do it at the same level of quality as the major brands.

Number two, by providing this value, the brands are taking the first step toward building a relationship with these potential customers. And not just any potential customers, but highly targeted ones. Who do you think is searching for content about painting a bedroom? That's right—someone who is about to paint their bedroom. By providing this content, Home Depot is positioning itself as the expert to a potential buyer in need. If that buyer watches a video from Home Depot that they find valuable about painting their room, who do you think they are going to give first crack at selling them the supplies to go do that job? That's right, Home Depot. It's just human nature to repay people when they provide you with value first. This is the ultimate case of win-win for both sides.

Or what if you're a tax software company, such as TurboTax or TaxAct? You could run expensive commercials on how you're the best tax solution or how you can deliver the lowest price. If you've ever been online as tax day approaches in April, you know that this is exactly the strategy that most of these companies take, spending hundreds of millions of dollars in the process.

But what if they focused on value instead? What if they created content that helped people out of a jam? Most people hate doing their taxes, mainly because they don't understand all of the pieces and it feels like a big headache. What if you created quality content that helped them navigate this process? Not an ad or infomercial, but valuable information that explained and simplified complex elements or gave them "life hacks" to save time or money in the process. Then you could use your substantial media dollars to promote these valuable videos and help push them to the top of the algorithms. Wouldn't this be a better use of your money than traditional ads?

This is how to think about content on YouTube. Just remember that your content on YouTube should always serve a purpose, one that is *valuable to your audience*. And most important, one that can be searched.

2. YouTube Technicalities

Now that you understand the philosophy of what works on YouTube, let's talk about the technical side. If you want your content to be found, you need to do the heavy lifting on the front end to make sure it can be searched. I could write an entire book about the technical side of social media, and this may be valuable for companies spending millions of dollars and creating thousands of content variants, but for most of those people reading this book, this would be incredibly tedious and boring, and 90 percent of that information would not be relevant. So I'm going to focus on the key technical details that you can utilize to make your own content more successful on YouTube. Specifically, I'm going to talk about the metadata that is crucial in maximizing your search results. If you're not familiar with it, metadata is a set of digital data that characterizes keywords, titles, authors, and other information for the purpose of identifying and indexing content. Think of the categorization on YouTube like the Dewey Decimal System that libraries use. Before the Dewey Decimal System was created in 1876, books were shelved based on their arrival date, which made finding books on any particular subject impossibly time-consuming. The new Dewey Decimal System, which organizes books based on subject matter, was a big improvement.

YouTube basically works the same way. Rather than organizing videos by the date they were posted, from newest to oldest, it slots them into categories based on the metadata provided by the poster and the content of the video.

When you upload a video to YouTube, two main assets go into the creation of that video as a piece of content. The first is the actual video itself. The second part is the metadata that YouTube uses to index videos. The metadata includes title, description, tags (which are keywords that describe the contents of the video for search), and the thumbnail (the primary still image that viewers see when your video pops up in their search).

All of these factors are taken into account and weighed by the YouTube algorithm to determine where in its vast library your video will be placed. Understanding how this is processed and cataloged is extremely important. The metadata on each video not only dictates search results, but it also helps determine what pops up in the recommended feed. This is the box on the right side of your YouTube desktop page, and it's critical to your success because it's literally the viewer's portal to the rabbit hole. The algorithm will recommend videos that it believes users may be interested in, based on what they have typed into the search box or what they have watched in the past.

Let's say you are a cooking influencer and you want to share your grandmother's amazing risotto recipe with the world. What are the key metadata components? Here are some simple dos and don'ts:

THE HEADLINE

YouTube calls this a title, but "headline" is the more appropriate term.

* Don't forget to name your video. You'd be surprised how many videos are out there with titles like "Risotto edit 3." And when you do name it, don't use some bland, generic headline like "Risotto Recipe." That doesn't explain what makes *your* video distinct from any of the other risotto recipes out there, so no one will click on it. Also, don't start making clickbait headlines like "Exploding Risotto" or silly things like that, unless you are actually blowing up risotto and filming it with a slow-motion camera. In that case, explain that in the headline!

* Make your headline unique, clear, and descriptive, such as "How to cook a perfect risotto 4 ways. My Italian grandmother's secret recipe revealed!" Of course, you should look at the competition in the category and see what has worked for them. You want to use keywords that have generated high traffic, and you want those words at the start of the title. If you have branding

or episode numbers or other un-catchy details that have to be included, they need to go at the end. You should also test your headline to determine exactly what options will resonate the most. (More on that in the next chapter.)

THE THUMBNAIL

* Pick an image you happen to like from the video. And never, ever allow the YouTube algorithm to select the image for you. It puts zero effort into this and it selects at random. You might as well be pulling options out of a hat blindfolded, and that's not a way to select what will drive people to click.
* Put as much thought into the thumbnail as you have into the rest of the video. Use a still photographer, or at least a decent camera, to capture beautiful and eye-catching images that will make for a distinctive thumbnail. That doesn't mean a freeze frame from your video won't work; in fact, sometimes it will still be the best option. The key is that you put the time in to find an image that will grab attention.

THE DESCRIPTION

* Don't make it generic or thoughtless. The first few words are absolutely key to making people watch, and the rest is the key to keeping them engaged. Repeating the headline and then dumping a bunch of tags and links underneath won't make anyone click anywhere.
* Remember your audience. In this case, they are probably out looking for risotto recipes, and you have the best one! You are a match made in heaven, provided you make them understand that, and fast! Give them a brief summary up top, with all the things that would entice someone looking for *this* recipe to

check out your video. Is it fast, easy to make, a sure-fire way to not fail? What are the key components of your particular recipe that make it unique? Put these qualities up front. After that, give them more details, be personal, and don't forget to be helpful by providing shopping lists and written recipes. Tell them you will do that in the initial description, so they know that if they click on your video, you will make things easy for them.

THE TAGS

* Don't forget to add tags. They are key to how the search engine works. Tags help users find your video when they search the site. When users type keywords related to your tags, your video will appear in their search results. If you don't use the word "truffle" in your text anywhere, the people searching for truffle risotto recipes will never find you. Also, don't misspell or use generic, irrelevant tags. The word "great" won't get you anywhere, but the words "tasty" and "tastiest" might help, while a misspelled "tastyest" won't do zip.

* Use the platform to help define your terms. You have the world's largest-reach engine at your fingertips, so please look at what it suggests. It's as simple as searching for things related to your risotto recipe and watching the autocomplete suggestions that pop up. Is the word "instant" included? I bet it is. See if it applies to your video. Maybe it should even be in the headline? From the word "instant," what other keywords can you glean? People want to make risotto "fast" using a "5-minute recipe," perhaps? This is also where the algorithm can be very useful; it is perfectly designed to extract tags from your video and from your competition. Take a look at the Keyword Suggestion Tool. Also, do include your name or brand name. This is surprisingly often overlooked, but you want peo-

ple searching for you to find your content, so add away. And one last thing: pull all your tags into a spreadsheet so that you can sort them by relevance. All the words and phrases that include "instant" or "fast" should be grouped together, so that you can determine your core choices. You just don't want to add hundreds of tags: you want to make sure you are adding the best and most relevant ones, and you want to make sure your very best ones are at the top of the list. Pulling them into a spreadsheet can be really helpful.

These steps will give you a good start, but remember, YouTube is the archive library of online video and your content can have a second life at any time, so keep all your metadata fresh by updating it periodically.

And please, at the risk of sounding like a dusty old schoolteacher, pretty please with sugar on top: Check your work! Failing to proofread is a sad reality and, amazing as it sounds, people will work for weeks on a video and then post it with a typo in the headline.

Of course, throughout all this, the most important thing to remember is to stick to your voice and to be authentic. There was a trend a few years back where people would try to game the system by adding keywords that were hot search topics at the time but had nothing to do with the video. It worked for a while, but YouTube clamped down on this practice pretty hard, punishing posters and even taking down videos that tried to ride trends that had nothing to do with their videos. Since then, the algorithm has changed, and if you try stunts like that now, the system will slap your fingers and punish you by dropping you in the rankings or blocking your video altogether.

When used in the right way, and with an authentic voice, YouTube can be a wonderful place for people to discover your content, the same way someone might find this book in their nearest public library.

Facebook: The Town Square

We spent a lot of time on YouTube and for good reason. It was the first platform, and in our imaginary city, this public library was the first building ever constructed. Everything else has, in one way or another, been built in response to it. We will go through the other platforms in just as much depth, but much quicker, because we've now established our reference point.

So, if YouTube is the public library, Facebook is the bustling, cobblestoned town square just outside it. This place is so pivotal and so ingrained in our society that we take much of its offerings for granted, even as new stores keep popping up faster than the old ones are closing. Yesterday, it was a peaceful square where we could reconnect with friends, but now it has a movie theater in Facebook Watch, it has a set of phone booths through Facebook Messenger, a market through Facebook Marketplace, and the dating apps are being installed as I type.

In many ways, Facebook is the exact opposite of YouTube. You leave the relative quiet of the library and step into a busy square jammed with people from all walks of life, happily shouting their opinions from every corner, eager to show you their food, the event they are going to attend on Thursday, or the pictures from the fabulous vacation they are having.

In short, while YouTube is an archive with a very long tail, Facebook is all about the immediate experience, about what's in your face right now. That's because it's a feed-based system. This is a fundamentally different beast, and one that many social media platforms have adopted. The concept is self-explanatory: When you open up

Facebook, Instagram, or Twitter, for example, what you see is your "feed." This is the stream of content that the algorithm has decided to put in front of you, based on whatever criteria you have established over time.

On Facebook, if you liked one of Lisa's posts, the algorithm will be slightly more prone to show you more posts from her over time. If you continue liking them, more and more will follow, and before long, you'll be living in a Lisa-centric bubble. This topic has been the cause of much debate, and Facebook is actively trying to change the algorithm to counteract this phenomenon. They are making progress, but to some extent the problem here is not one of Facebook's making, but rather one of human nature.

Say you are walking through the town square to your favorite coffee shop, and there's a loud gathering outside. Perhaps it's a bunch of people who have opinions different from yours on some passionate topic, and they happen to be screaming their ideas at one another. Wouldn't you rather go to another coffee shop, so you can have a quiet moment to catch up with your friends?

Of course you would, as would most people. We'd all rather sit in peace and quiet with our friends to chat, happy in our own little bubble, than to confront and deal with a loud crowd.

This act of human nature, when extrapolated into the Facebook algorithm, means that if you are a left-wing liberal, you are very unlikely to see conservative viewpoints in your feed. We are very quick to point the finger at Facebook for this problem, as if they were somehow actively trying not to let us see the other side, when the reality is that we actually *choose* not to see it. We *choose* to sit in the coffee shop across the square.

Of course, the square is also littered with all kinds of propaganda. There are people who are actually robots in disguise, telling us to have opinions about anything from world politics to brand-new hand towels. Because we aren't used to robots yet, we still tend to mistake them for real people. The algorithm is learning how to spot them as well, so the only real advice here is to be aware when you wander around the place. Some people really aren't what they appear, and some aren't even people at all.

The square is also an excellent place to hide in plain sight. Think of it like the proverbial water cooler at work, the gathering place where people stop to exchange stories from their lives, talk sports, politics, or entertainment. The big difference here is that as you entered this square, you were handed a magical cloak, straight out of J.R.R. Tolkien, giving you the power of invisibility. You can step right up to the water cooler, listen in on conversations, and never even reveal that you were there. Again, this comes down to one's choice. It's only when you *choose* to engage that you must take your cloak off and reveal yourself.

So what does all this mean if you are looking to step into this noisy and loud and busy place and somehow break through? It means you need to grab attention. Something big and loud and eye-catching that makes everyone in the square suddenly turn their heads to look. It won't last long, no matter what you do. Facebook posts have a far more dynamic spike than videos uploaded to YouTube. Views, reactions, and shares come quickly after a post and then typically drop off significantly over the first week or two, or until you repost the content in the future.

This is all because of the Facebook feed-based system. As soon as your post hits someone's feed, something else is coming right behind it, ready to gobble up their attention. Everything on Facebook is a flash in the pan, come and gone in an instant. But that doesn't make it any less efficient — actually, quite the opposite.

Because Facebook is driven so heavily by the algorithm, rather than by human input into a search field, you can tailor your content to be hyper-efficient with your audience. The audience segmentation tools on Facebook are unparalleled. When the time comes to zero in on who should see your message, no other platform (with the exception of Instagram, which is owned by Facebook) comes close.

This means a number of things, all of which fit into the concept of full funnel marketing. Funnel marketing, simply put, is the idea that you grab massive awareness at the top of the funnel to make everyone know you exist, then you guide people down the funnel with more engaging content, and ultimately convert them, meaning you drive some of them to take an action, such as signing up for a newsletter or buying a pair of shoes, whatever your goal may be.

The way we think about this, for Facebook in particular, has a number of interesting and unique differentiators. I will walk you through three detailed examples to demonstrate this.

1. The Traditional Funnel

The top of the funnel is massive awareness. Traditionally this was done through TV, radio, and print ads. You simply spend a lot of money and plaster the town and the airwaves with your branding, so that when people think of your product category, you are top of mind. This used to be very effective, and if you have bazillions of dollars you can still go this route; it just happens to cost more and tends to be less effective these days.

On social media, the rules are different. The core idea — that you need awareness and attention — still holds true, but where you used to have to indiscriminately blast your message across the rooftops in order to reach as many people as possible, you can now *target* your awareness campaigns and aim them directly at the precise audience that you want to sell to.

Let's say you are the Ford Motor Company and you want to sell the brand-new Mustang. In the old world you would buy a Super Bowl ad and a bunch of prime-time television commercials, plus radio and print ads in all the glossy places, and your message would be seen by everyone. But these days, these questions need to be asked: How many of the people you are reaching are in the market for a new car? How many are in the market for a muscle car? How many of those also happen to like American cars over all the European or Asian competitors? The percentage is heartbreakingly small. That means you have spent millions of dollars putting your message in front of people who will never in a million years buy the car. Even if they *love* the ad you made, it doesn't change the fact that they may already have a brand-new car, or they are only halfway through their current lease, or they hate muscle cars, or they are looking for a mini-van to cart the kids around to soccer practice.

Bottom line? That's a lot of advertising money poorly spent.

2. The Social Media Funnel

On social media, and in particular with Facebook and Instagram, you can create a hyper-targeted and segmented audience. To start, you define your core audience by setting parameters in four different categories:

I. DEMOGRAPHIC

Age, gender, relationship status, education, workplace, job titles, and more. This is the first and most basic step in segmentation.

II. LOCATION

Geographic area targeting, down to a radius around any specific location of your choosing. Want to reach people at Wrigley Field? Create a custom radius and only target people in that specific area.

III. INTERESTS

Cluster groups of people based on what they like, their hobbies, favorite movies and TV shows, leisure activities, and more. Selling hiking backpacks? Zero in on people who like camping, hiking, and outdoor sports.

IV. BEHAVIORS

You can customize your audience down to specific purchase behaviors, such as what device they like to use and a whole host of other activities. Selling an app that's available only on Android? Skip iOS users with a click.

Of course, the more targeted your audience is, the more expensive they are to reach. This is because of the auction-based media system on most social media platforms. We will dive into this in more depth in Chapter 9, but it's important to understand the basics here.

Auction-Based Media: An Overview

On traditional media, all ads are created equal. If you are spending $300K to place your 30-second spot in an episode of *The Big Bang Theory,* the network really doesn't care what your ad is, how good or bad it is, or what the audience might think about it — it's still going to cost you the same. The networks care only that your ad is not offensive and that it meets their standards and practices for broadcast, including any FCC regulations — but they do not have any opinion on the creativity or effectiveness of your ad. Want to spend $5M on a Super Bowl spot that has an action sequence full of explosions or simply text on black? Producing them might have different price tags, but the Super Bowl media buy is the same.

But on social media, it's all the exact opposite.

Remember, these platforms are created for their *users,* not for advertisers. Selling eyeballs is an add-on, not a core mission. Because of this, social media platforms are most interested in serving their audience. That means if their audience doesn't like your ad, the engagement and view time will be low and you will be kicked lower in the algorithm, meaning they will charge you more money per view to serve the ad. Conversely, if people are engaging with your video, it will rise in the algorithm and become cheaper to serve as an ad (which we will cover in the next chapter).

We will go into more detail on this later, but for now it's important to understand this core principal of how media buying works on social media, so that you can maximize your content for the different platforms.

This is especially important on Facebook, simply because it has been around longer than any other feed-based platform. That means the algorithm has had more time to develop and mature, making it more and more sophisticated over time.

On Facebook you can select a very narrow target audience, but go too small and your impact will be limited. This is simple math. If you give your content to 100 million people and 1 percent like it, that's a million people! If you narrow your audience size down to Wrigley Field, that's only 40,000 people if the ballpark is sold out, and how many of them check Facebook through the game? Okay, probably half of them, let's call it 20,000 people. If 1 percent of that audience likes your content, well, that's only 200 people.

The way you want to play this game depends entirely on what your objectives are. But it's important to understand what drives the platform in order to intelligently pick an audience that is right for you.

Now, this only touches the top of the social media funnel. Once you have created a big sonic boom to get everyone's attention, it's time to start pushing them down the funnel toward conversion, and this is where the audience segmentation and targeting get really interesting.

Let's say you got a million views on your video. Great work. Now let's look at what these numbers really mean, and, more important, what real numbers are hiding behind them . . .

As mentioned in Chapter 3, Facebook counts anyone stopping for 3 seconds or more as a view. They will give you retention data on top of this, meaning how long people stuck around to watch — but they can't tell if that's because someone stopped scrolling because they went to the bathroom or if they were really watching, so it's very hard to quantify these metrics.

The only real way to determine if someone really leaned in is the engagement metrics. Remember, this is the measure of people who actively choose to react to, comment on, or share your video. The Golden Benchmark is 1 percent; the median for best-in-class on the Ad Age Viral Leaderboard in 2017 was 0.87 percent.

Let's say you beat out all the big brands, all the Pepsis and Nikes of the world, and your video had a whopping 1 percent engagement rate — that means 10,000 people cared enough to react, share, or comment. That sounds like a small number out of the 1 million, but this is where the audience segmentation becomes intriguing.

As you analyze the people who interacted with your content, you will discover audience patterns that may not have been obvious at the outset. Perhaps your content is performing better with young women in Wisconsin than you could have imagined, or perhaps it really resonates with people who like fishing? Whatever the details are, Facebook can extract them for you, and you can now create *look-alike audiences* based on those criteria. That means that from the 10,000 people you have found to be primed for your content, you can now extrapolate millions more who share some key parameters. When you serve your ad to this new group, you will have a much better chance of engaging them.

This becomes especially important when it comes to conversion. At Shareability, our methodology is to create conversion assets with *visual thematics* that connect viewers to the awareness campaign. By retargeting this content to *prior engagers* — meaning those people who engaged with the awareness content as well as their look-alike audiences — we then trigger a sense of recognition and satisfaction in people's minds. This connection makes them far more likely to take action.

Of course, we design the action based on the needs of our clients, meaning we can drive people to click through to a website, or check out more content, or learn about a product, or head off to a store with the intent to purchase.

This mechanism also makes Facebook one of the strongest options for product discovery. Because the feed is inherently a bubble filled with our friends, we tend to trust it. As marketers, we can tap into this trust and allow people to discover our products through their feed. By serving up reliable product information, we can allow people to conveniently check out a product and start to make up their own mind. Once we see who's interested, we can then retarget them and build more look-alike audiences.

3. The Reverse Funnel

Because we live and breathe this space every day, we have a unique point of view. (If you've seen the show *Stranger Things*, it's sort of like how Eleven describes the Upside Down. If you haven't seen the show, then go check it out, it's great, but in the meantime you can think of it as a parallel world where everything is backward and upside-down, like a fun-house-mirror reflection of our reality.) This point of view allows us to look at ordinary things in an extraordinary way, especially when it comes to bucking the deeply rooted trends of traditional media and advertising.

As we looked at the traditional sales funnel, it struck us that it should be flipped on its head. Now, as a primary tool, the traditional funnel still serves a great purpose, but as an additional angle of attack. In order to explain this, let's look at a recent client of ours, TaxAct.

TaxAct is a software services solution for people who file their own taxes. They are a challenger brand, coming in at fourth place against the established behemoths of TurboTax, H&R Block, and Credit Karma. When we first spoke to them, they were 100 percent focused on a traditional TV campaign for the 2019 tax season. They had a significant media budget and considerable TV commercial production budgets. They were planning to develop traditional TV spots to drive awareness, pushing those spots not only on broadcast but also as pre-roll ads on social media. They were looking for creative ideas and talking to a number of traditional agencies.

We had no interest in competing in the traditional space and didn't really understand why we were asked to participate, but we were told they were open to doing something different. We threw caution to the wind and played it straight, all cards on the table. We explained how we operate, how our process is totally different from traditional TV, and then we suggested a revolutionary approach to *arrive* at their TV ads. It was a three-pronged strategy.

I. DIGITAL-FIRST ARCHITECTURE

Our digital-first mindset means we create all of our content on and for digital, using that as a testing ground, making sure our concepts are resonating with an audience before taking them to traditional media such as TV and print.

II. TEST AND OPTIMIZE MESSAGING

The messaging—telling people what you stand for—is just as important on digital as in traditional advertising, but the difference is that testing your messaging in a traditional way generally involves focus groups or very small sample groups. By testing our messaging on Facebook, we can dial in much more finely tuned results through our proprietary Test & Learn process where we A/B-test different creative variants with real audiences on Facebook.

III. FULL FUNNEL CONVERSION

This is the natural conclusion of the reverse funnel. The results we arrive at will be implemented in a tried-and-tested full funnel marketing approach, including all the advancements that Facebook has to offer, creating a much more trackable consumer journey.

Put another way, we are testing our content on digital to make sure it hits all the right notes *before* our client spends millions of dollars buying TV ads, only to discover it may or may not work. This is a much more logical and methodical way of approaching creative content, and it helps yield incredible results. And it helped us win the TaxAct business.

Facebook Technical Overview

Remember, the biggest technical difference between Facebook and YouTube is the feed-based nature of the platform. In addition to all the details already mentioned, this also means that you can aggregate other users' content without fear of repercussion or ill will. If you do that on YouTube, you basically have to rip off someone else's video and upload it as your own, which is inherently stealing, and neither the community or the platform will reward you. On the other hand, with Facebook, people are excited to share their content, and when they do, your content literally ends up in their outgoing feed, and it becomes part of their story. That is what makes Facebook so powerful—you are essentially creating brand ambassadors out of your audience.

This also works in reverse. You can like and share and engage with content on the platform, and when these actions end up in *your* feed, they become part of *your* narrative. That means your feed is not just your original content, but also a slate of aggregated content. This enables you to create pages that are inherently active and have high engagement, which helps the algorithms when you launch your own content. Because you seem to be engaging with an audience, the algorithm will have a natural *bias* toward promoting your work. It's a positive spiral that you can own and control—by understanding this, you will become more or less immune to algorithm changes.

Consider when Facebook tightened the funnel on postings by limiting the amount of posts from each user in 2018. The amount of organic traffic that people were receiving on their posts went down. BuzzFeed may have been used to 40 percent of their audience seeing everything they posted; now it dropped to 25 percent. That's cutting their reach almost in half.

But for the brands who understand Facebook, these kinds of changes shouldn't matter. The best content on Facebook will perform at the same level *regardless* of changes in the algorithm. The same principles always apply. Sure, the floor and ceiling may contract a bit, but the best content is always going to outperform all the rest. Facebook will always grade on a curve in terms of what the existing conditions are, and as long as you are in step with the big picture, you will consistently outperform others trying to do what you're doing.

In addition to this, there are myriad other small but vital details to consider when creating content for the social media platforms. Here are the most important ones.

i. Openings

Creating engaging content is essential on Facebook, and nothing has greater impact on your video than the first few seconds. Think of the town square again, and imagine yourself browsing for a store to visit. What makes you choose which one to enter? Sure, if you are shopping for shoes, you might not stop at the bakery, but what if that yummy pastry in the window looks amazing? What if they have a friendly staff member outside, handing out samples to whet your appetite? Maybe you could stop in for just a minute, a quick drink and a snack won't kill anyone? It might just be the boost you need to get you through all the important shoe shopping you have to do . . .

This "barker" outside the store is the first 3, 5, and 7 seconds of your video. It's what stops you as you are scrolling through your daily feed. If the video you are rushing past begins with text on black, or some mundane landscape shots with boring music underneath, will that tempt you to check out the rest of it? Probably not. In fact, odds are you will never know what that video was supposed to be about in the first place. But if your video begins with an attention-grabbing headline combined with a great visual, you'll be hooked and will be sure to check out what the video has to offer.

ii. Sound

Sound, or rather the *absence* of sound, is pivotal. An astounding 85 percent of Facebook users will scroll through their feed with the sound *off.* They might be at work, on the bus, in a meeting, or on the toilet; no matter where they are, the odds are very high they will not have any audio to go along with your video. This means your content must be enjoyable, clear, and concise *without any sound whatsoever.*

Therefore, absolutely compelling text is mandatory. Not just subtitles, which are a must, but also big blocks of text to help explain the narrative. At Shareability, we routinely bake both types of text into our video, meaning we don't even rely on Facebook's native subtitling engine, but prefer to make sure our subtitles can't be turned off.

Of course, if your audience turns their sound on, that needs to be enjoyable as well. We take great pains to maximize the experience of sound on our videos because the people who will turn the sound on are often those with whom your video is resonating the most, your highest engagers. You need to make them as happy as, or happier than, the casual viewer.

iii. Mobile

One of the most important things to remember is that 90 percent of Facebook's daily users access the platform via mobile. This is huge in terms of how you program content for these viewers. There are three operational steps we always use to ensure our content plays well on mobile:

1. GO VERTICAL — The standard aspect ratio of modern video is 16 x 9, the same aspect ratio that any modern TV set has. Going vertical means flipping that sideways, making the image taller than it is wide by an aspect ratio of 9 x 16. While this is perfectly native for lots of platforms, and Facebook actually recommends it, we have developed our own proprietary format that we tend to prefer, something we call the Shareability Vertical. We looked at the interface on Facebook, especially based on the fact that we prioritize engagements, and we designed an aspect ratio that leaves just enough space for the icons that signify engagement actions (that is, reactions, comments, and shares), so that these actions are always available to the user, even in full screen. This aspect ratio works out as 1 x 1.25, meaning

the frame is 1.25 times as tall as it is wide. In simplest terms, we found that this is the best size ratio for viewing on a mobile phone.

This works well inside the feed, not just in full screen, as it creates a better viewing experience for the user, keeping them engaged for a longer period of time, leading to better engagements. It also helps hide the next post in their feed, helping to minimize distractions.

It's important to note that we still shoot almost all of our videos in the traditional 16 x 9 format because we deliver not just on Facebook but on YouTube and other platforms as well. You don't need to *capture* vertical in order to deliver it, but you do need to be mindful of it as you go through production to make sure you are covering all aspect ratios for all of your intended delivery formats and platforms.

In addition, you can transform a 16 x 9 aspect ratio to square, or to our Shareability Vertical, by using what's known as a meme box. This is essentially the placement of bars at the top and bottom, ranging from simple black to any color or image you like, where the top bar has a captivating message that places the video in context and the bottom bar houses the subtitles.

2. PICK A DYNAMIC THUMBNAIL — Many people assume that thumbnails don't matter on Facebook because the video starts playing as soon as you scroll to it, but that is simply inaccurate. If you are on desktop, you might be able to see three or more posts on a single page, but only one of these videos will play. On mobile there is an option to turn off autoplay when not connected to Wi-Fi, to save on data. That means your thumbnail has to be captivating enough for someone to actually click on it before it starts to play.

3. OPTIMIZE TEXT — You are already using text to communicate with those watching with the sound off, but now you have to make that text bigger, bolder, and more in-your-face so that it stands out at a glance on a tiny mobile screen. This often means breaking the

rules of graphic design in order to get your message across, but if you are a graphic designer at heart, you should stop and ask yourself what's more important: that the text looks "right" to you, or that people actually read it. I hope it's the latter.

Another important element is the *post text optimization*. This is the text that accompanies the video in the feed. It informs the viewer of what they will be getting into and why they should engage. This text is pivotal, because viewers will often read this *at the same time* as they are absorbing the first few frames of your video, and if they don't process the two together in a positive way, they will simply move on.

Remember to keep this text very short and to the point. We've found the optimal length of post text is a mere 6 to 9 words. Wherever possible, avoid using links in the post text, which take users off the platform. This, we've observed, will not only affect watch time, but will negatively influence the organic reach of the post. If you need to link anywhere, use a native link button, such as a "learn more" activation, for example.

Instagram: The Art Gallery

Adjacent to the town square of Facebook in our internet city, we find the art gallery, also known as Instagram. While you might look at Instagram and feel like it's somehow raw or unpolished, the similarities to a fine art gallery are deeper than you might think.

Think of what gets displayed in the Louvre, or the Met — not just any old painting will make the cut. These are the museums of only the finest works of art, carefully selected by curators and committees, occasionally with some specific piece on display that stands out, perhaps muscled in by a well-paying sponsor.

If we translate all of this into the digital world of Instagram, the work of art on display is there to showcase the absolute best version of ourselves. People don't post their anxieties or fears on this platform — those are for the conversations in the Facebook town square. On Instagram, it's all about holding up a truly polished image of ourselves, to show all the best aspects of our lives, or our brand.

Where the library of YouTube explores deep topics and complex instructions on things like how to assemble garden gnomes, these posts are all about evocative aesthetics. While you might go to YouTube to find out how to make the best chocolate cake by watching a fairly detailed video that gives you all the necessary steps, on Instagram there won't be any steps or directions, just a picture of the best-looking chocolate cake ever.

If a picture is truly worth a thousand words, with more than 30 billion pictures shared, Instagram is home to 30 *trillion* words. This makes Instagram *the* place for *visual storytelling*. This is powerful because it gives both people and brands the ability to tell their stories through imagery, offering their audience a window to see the world through somebody else's eyes and to encounter images that evoke a strong human connection.

Because Instagram started as a photo-based feed, with video becoming what is now an inevitable afterthought, the video requirements are different than on other platforms. Unlike YouTube and Facebook, Instagram caps their video length at 60 seconds. Because it's primarily a visual medium, with a real premium on the quality of the visuals, more experiential or visceral content does not perform as well, while evocative or more glossy imagery does better on Instagram than on Facebook.

Instagram's integration with Facebook (which started in 2012, when Facebook acquired Instagram) means that the same type of targeting can happen, but the user interface is different, and that changes some of the core fundamentals. Whereas Facebook is great for that sonic boom, Instagram is more of a niche platform. On Facebook, an audience that likes a certain item will also have other interests on the platform because the content available is so varied — between friends and family, articles and shopping, not to mention all the ads they are reacting to. In other words, the information flow on Facebook is fairly broad.

On Instagram, however, there is a much narrower window. People who like esoteric jokes will keep liking esoteric jokes and people who like pictures of cats will continue to like pictures of cats. No one will stop to read an article or watch a long-form video about some completely different subject matter. In other words, they are in the art gallery to see some art, and they are really not interested in anything else.

As Instagram rose in popularity, the feature set was expanded, moving into direct competition with other platforms. Instagram stories, for example, are a direct attack on Snapchat, as they are exactly the kind of content that Snapchat has. For brands, this has become an opportunity because it allows them to drive people to longer videos and even to digital storefronts. In a push to have brands use their posts for conversion, Instagram shops now allow brands to display prices for their products on the platform.

Instagram also opened a two-way conversation between brands and consumers. The incorporation of "stickers" into Instagram stories allows consumers to provide direct input to a brand, thus allowing followers to feel more engaged in that brand and the choices they offer.

Succeeding on Instagram is all about decluttering your message. You need to tell your story in a clear, concise, and visually pleasing way. Any aesthetically pleasing post will draw engagement, just like a beautiful painting in an art gallery. On Instagram, you are asking someone to appreciate that image, and if they really do appreciate it, they might take the next step and comment on it. If the image triggers an emotional response or it makes a real connection with the viewer, then they might dig further into your other content.

As Instagram has evolved, the platform has allowed users to move beyond a simple act of appreciation to actual engagement, primarily through Instagram stories and swipe-up features that allow users to post comments. In the past, the site offered more of a shallow interaction, but these more recent changes are driving them from a simple appreciation of an image to more detailed storytelling.

Of course, all of this is rooted in the core premise of keeping people around long enough to show their appreciation, but it all begins with the initial visual. If someone is following an account or a brand, and the posting suddenly stops being visually engaging, they will unfollow the account and never find out the full story the brand wants to tell them.

Know this: Building followers on Instagram is extremely difficult and time-consuming, so your biggest focus should be on finding a very specific voice and style that potential audiences will find valuable. In other words, people follow accounts on Instagram looking for a very specific value proposition. That could range from X to Y. Just remember that once you've found that value proposition, any variance or deviation from that voice will be not well received. I've actually experienced an extreme case of this myself when I started working with the great soccer star Ronaldo.

Although I view Instagram as one of the great marketing platforms for the next ten years, I don't consider it as the most relevant platform for my personal brand, so I hardly ever post. When Shareability started working with Cristiano Ronaldo, he started following me on Instagram. With one click of his finger, I was inundated with followers who viewed me as someone who was relevant in Ronaldo's sphere. Ronaldo has over 140 million followers on Instagram, more than anyone in the world, and when he followed me, my phone exploded with follower notifications and it really hasn't stopped since.

All of a sudden I had tens of thousands of new followers. But all these followers came with their own agendas and expectations. When I posted some pictures of Ronaldo, or of myself in his inner circle, I received thousands of engagements.

But when I then posted photos of my kids fishing?

Crickets.

Myself at a business conference?

Radio silence.

A picture of me with Ronaldo's manager?

Thousands of instant Likes.

The lesson here is that Instagram is a fickle beast. As long as you keep the audience engaged with the precise thing they came to you to see, the engagement can be amazing. But if you stray and start posting things they don't care about, they will unfollow you in droves.

Understanding the philosophy of Instagram is essential. And to do that, here are some tactical approaches that can be very useful.

i. Followers

For Instagram, start by knowing that building a big following is a high-wire balancing act. You need to post often enough to keep your audience's attention but not so much that they feel spammed and decide to block you. Generally speaking, we've found that you shouldn't make more than one post a day unless there is something really special to showcase. On average, a posting cadence of 2–3 times a week is the sign of a healthy channel. You can post more, but once you start, be prepared to keep it up. Accounts that abruptly decrease their post frequency lose followers quickly.

ii. Hashtags

Hashtags are an extremely important part of the Instagram community. Not only are they used to help creators categorize their content and to define their brand, they also allow users to explore new content. Each hashtag has an ever-changing collection of "top posts." When a user clicks on a hashtag, these top posts are displayed first and can lead to additional followers and more engagement.

iii. Instagram Stories

This is a direct jab at Snapchat, using posts that vanish after 24 hours. It's the complete opposite of the YouTube library; that is, these are like pop-up art installations, and if you miss them while they're in town, too bad. They are a once-in-a-lifetime experience, here today, gone tomorrow, and gone forever.

Much like pop-up experiences in real life, they are also located in a separate location. They don't show up on your profile grid or in the main Instagram feed. Instead they appear in a bar at the top of your feed. All Instagram accounts can share stories, from your best friend's birthday party to your favorite celebrity's movie premiere. When a new story goes live, their profile photo will light up with a colorful ring around it, drawing your eye and attention and almost instinctively making you want to tap it.

This is great for marketers. At first it might seem that all the effort that goes into creating our content would somehow be wasted on something that will simply vanish in 24 hours. But because of the instant and immediate attention, it often drives traffic in incomparable numbers, and it's an opportunity to create a Facebook-style sonic boom inside the art gallery of Instagram.

As a side note, Facebook is of course rolling out Facebook Stories, which is basically the exact same thing, only back out in the town square. We all know the art installations inside the "real" art gallery have more credibility, so I don't expect the Facebook version to be nearly as popular.

Once the user taps someone's story, it appears full screen (meaning all your deliverables need to be full vertical, the 9 x 16 aspect ratio) and all the content posted will play in chronological order. Users can move backward and forward through the story, and they can swipe to another person's story the very second they become bored with yours.

Unlike regular posts, there are no Likes or public comments, meaning that there is no feedback activity for the audience, making this highly of-the-moment activity somewhat passive, which reduces attention spans. The trick here is to be brief and entertaining. Usually we find that a total runtime of under 60 seconds is ideal. Give it a try, play around with it, and see what resonates with your audience.

Direct Messaging Systems: The Post Office

Last but not least is the post office. Every city or town needs a delivery system for mail, packages, and consumer products. Our internet city has many different services that fit this description, each a little bit different, all offering various add-ons. You should consider the direct messaging service an add-on to their core functionality.

For the purposes of this exercise, Snapchat, Twitter, WhatsApp, and Facebook Messenger are all part of the direct messaging ecosystem.

The medium may vary, but the goal is the same: sending messages directly between people. Could be from one person to another, or between a specific group of people. The messages can be text, photos, videos, GIFs, memes, or any type of media, even good old-fashioned attachments.

The big difference comes in the specific usage. You need to treat these delivery systems differently, the same as you would treat the US Post Office, FedEx, or a local courier differently. If something is more sacred and close to home, and you need it to arrive safely or in a timely fashion, you might hire a local courier to deliver it. If it needs to be across the country by tomorrow morning, you go to FedEx. For all of your regular, basic stuff, you just throw a stamp on it and drop it in the mailbox.

Now, in this chapter, we've gone deep into YouTube, Facebook, and Instagram. I emphasize those three because I feel that these are the best platforms for brands and personalities to build their influence and to break through the noise. Conversely, I don't feel that direct messaging platforms are the right place for you to build your brand. Yes, they can be an amazing tool, but in my experience, they are much more apt for big corporations with lots of resources and lots of workers and AI computing power ready to drive messaging home to customers.

It's also inherently difficult to gain traction and to build a loyal following through direct messaging. The core idea is built around one-to-one or one-to-a-few messaging, and that's really not a forum for mass communication. That's not to say that it can't be done, but I wouldn't recommend that you even try until you've mastered the big three platforms that I've outlined above.

I strongly believe that you will get a lot better return for your time and money on YouTube, Facebook, and Instagram, so I won't go into the direct messaging platforms in any great depth.

All this being said, I'll leave you with some thoughts regarding Twitter. Though the platform is not a fire-starter to ignite content, it can be a very useful live-engagement platform to check the pulse of the internet. It's also much more of a two-way street, a very immediate place for the here and now. This makes it an effective place for small brands to build one-on-one relationships and to position themselves in their particular industry.

Some brands use Twitter as customer service, or to establish a direct dialogue with their customers. Or they communicate via Twitter with their customers who are having issues. For example, if someone is stuck on the tarmac for hours on a flight, they will tweet this news, thereby causing the airline to respond with compensation or with an explanation for the delay.

Brands that use Twitter most effectively do so in the voice of the platform and talk to people in bite-sized phrases, and never in long sentences. The fast-food chain Wendy's has been particularly good at this. They used Twitter to change the way they talk to their customers. Instead of being a passive brand, they adopted an edgier, irreverent voice that spoke to their customers who wanted something relatable and different. Here is a classic:

Customer: "Hey, Wendy's, my friend wants to go to McDonald's. What should I tell him?"

Wendy's: "Find new friends."

That's how you do Twitter.

The Other Platforms

There are other small, yet important platforms that we don't widely use for branding. LinkedIn, for example, is not a content vehicle, but it may work for you. It has a very specific purpose. LinkedIn is used to market yourself to the business world, to upgrade your career, to build relationships, and to expand your network. LinkedIn is more valuable for individuals than it is for companies. Though there is a way to advertise to specific subsets and target companies, most people use it for interconnectivity and career building.

And there is Amazon, which was built to sell you stuff. Amazon is the biggest end-user platform in the world, and it is vitally important if you are retailing. However, it is also different because you don't technically create content for Amazon (other than a brief description and visuals of your product.) After you have established a relationship with a customer on the other platforms, if you are selling a product, you can then drive the customer to Amazon.

And there is Reddit. This is supposedly an impossible platform to crack (even though we have managed, through our John Cena campaign for Cricket). But even Reddit is opening up and becoming more brand-friendly, so it will certainly be an interesting space to keep an eye on in the near future.

There are numerous other platforms as well, with some closing or merging and new ones popping up all the time. The internet is a big city, and there's room for all kinds of services. Based on who you are and what type of business you are running, some will be more valuable than others, but no matter what the platform is, it all comes back to the same basic theme: your messaging and your relationship to your customers.

You have to find the inherent shareability of your brand in order to make anyone pay attention, on any platform.

Rule 9

Test Before You Invest

N ow it's time to make your content go boom. You understand the science of being shareable. You've focused on providing value. You've found your voice. You've crushed the headline. After listening to the internet, you've decided either to ride a wave or flip the script. You've taken a tour of internet city, studied the platforms, and decided which ones are right for your message.

After spending all this time (and likely some money), failure to launch properly is not an option. It would be like an airline building amazing lounges and a luxury check-in service but forgetting to train their pilots — a terrible idea, sure to end in a spectacular crash.

The groundwork has been laid and you have a solid foundation, but now it's time to take the most important step. To prevent your content from being that proverbial tree that falls in the forest without anybody hearing it, you will need to *test* before you invest. Testing is a key step in the process, and one that is traditionally completely overlooked or, at best, mismanaged. Doing this right will allow you to experiment and optimize your content *before* you go all in. If done correctly, it can not only bring you deep efficiencies, but can also have a massive impact on the overall success of your content.

This chapter will detail the specifics of testing, but before we get into the nitty-gritty, let's take a step back and talk about your packaging. Just like any other product, great content deserves great packaging. You wouldn't ship a luxury steak knife wrapped in an old sock in a cardboard box, so why would you treat your social content any differently?

Below I've outlined three interconnected principles that you need to understand to get your content packaged and ready for testing.

1. Make a Silent Film

According to Digiday, up to 85 percent of Facebook videos are viewed with the sound off: *85 percent*. Although that sounds like an unbelievable number (some people argue it is closer to 50 percent, but I'm skeptical), it actually makes sense, when you think about it. Most people watching videos on social media are doing so on their phone. Often this happens with other people around or in a public space. Nobody will turn their sound on in any of those situations. Take note of your own habits next time you scroll through your Facebook feed. I'm willing to bet that more often than not, you will do it with the sound off.

That means that in terms of pulling people into your video, you are essentially making a silent film. That's right, we are right back to the birth of cinema, where the visual is *everything*. This is a very important concept to understand when it comes to the packaging of your content, and you have to treat all of the elements of your film accordingly.

It's a fascinating concept. For all our technological advancements, and how much our habits of viewing and interacting with content have changed over the past 100 years, they have also stayed very much the same. On the internet, we are now basically back to where we started, in the silent film era of the early 1900s, when projectors were able to showcase the flicker of moving images, but no one had cracked how to add synchronized sound. Sure, there was a pianist on hand who gave you a live score, but dialogue was all delivered through text cards, *exactly the way we now do it on social media*. Who knows, maybe we will have an audio revolution as we did in cinemas in the late 1920s, when the "talkies" were created. Maybe aural implants or vibrating eyewear will bypass our biological limitations, and Instagram will be able to launch its own talkies in a few years.

Enough of the history lesson — what does this mean for your content? It means that you need to take Chapter 5 to heart and really crush the headline, so you draw people in. It means that you need to have an opening image, combined with graphics, that tells a very clear story about what the video is, without relying on sound or narration (more on that in point 2 below). And it means that you need to "give up the goat" and get to your best stuff quickly, so that you lay the hook and give yourself the best possible odds that your viewers will stick around (be sure to see point 3 below).

Always go through the process of watching your video with the sound off, and see how it feels and if the message and hook are communicated clearly. Once you feel good about it, show it to your friends, family, or coworkers who haven't yet seen it, and ask them to tell you what it was about. You will always be surprised at their first impression, and it will help you home in on and clarify your concept. Ask if the intro hooked them in and made them want to watch the rest, or if they would just keep scrolling if this popped up in their feed.

The toughest, and most important part of this process, is to actually take their answers to heart. You need to firmly believe in what the platforms all believe, which is that the gut reaction of the consumer is *always* king. You then need to keep adjusting your packaging until you're getting a consistent positive response. Remember that most people won't be paying attention to your content the way that you will. They will be casually scrolling past, and if your post happens to catch their eye, they might stick around and check it out, but they will *never* get precious with it. Neither should you. You need to be prepared to "kill your babies," as all filmmakers are told to do when they get obsessed with some detail that the audience doesn't care about. Just because you worked really hard at it doesn't make it any more valuable than the random thing most people seem to love. In fact, it's the thing people react to that is the most valuable of all.

The bottom line of all this is that *if* you can make your content hyper-appealing as a silent film, it will only get better when someone actually turns the sound on and makes it a talkie.

2. Marry Text and Images

When you're making a silent film, the text and images play a crucial role in delivering a clear message to your audience. In our work, we've become very proficient in a format we call the Shareability Social Editorial. It's part of the Shareability Matrix, which is an ever-evolving breakdown of formats and production approaches that work well on social media at any given time — it's also deep and complex enough to be the subject of a whole other book. For now, let's focus on the Shareability Social Editorial, a format that essentially tells a story in a *neutral third-person past-tense voice*. I know it sounds complicated, but think of it as telling a newspaper story in headlines, only the headlines happen to play over relevant video, and occasionally you will hear a quote from someone connected to the story.

This means we place headline-style copy in a clearly readable font over key visuals to tell the story in both words as well as pictures. In other words, we're telling the story using easy-to-understand headlines for those watching without sound.

The *neutral third-person* voice is important because it feels journalistic. It's essential to stay truthful and use this approach with integrity. The audience will instantly smell any falseness a mile away, so I'm in no way suggesting you "fake" the journalism. But that being said, you can adopt the neutral and observational tone of real and honest reporting. Third person is also a key component of all this, as it makes the message resonate much more truthfully. Rather than say "we wanted to" we would say "Adobe wanted to," for example. This distances the brand from the content, allowing the real people involved in the content to step up and be seen as the heroes. The brand is simply there to support them in their journey, a stance much more admirable than chest thumping.

The past tense is not only important because it makes the tone feel journalistic, but because quite frankly, it's easier to follow. We are simply retelling the story of something that already happened and holding this event up for the world to see. The past tense makes it easy to digest and retain.

This is not a patented approach in any way. Similar social editorial styles are utilized in varying degrees by many top digital publishers, including AJ+, Cheddar, BuzzFeed, and more recently, Facebook. If you look around the various social platforms, you will recognize this format quickly. I can virtually guarantee something along these lines will pop up in your feed today.

Because of its universal appeal, this format has produced some of the most viewed and shared content on the internet. When creating your own content, it is important to use language that feels familiar. That often means leaning into publishers that are relevant to the content you are creating. You also need to make sure the quality is a match. Most would think that means you need to make it snazzy, glossy, and polished, but often it's exactly the opposite. We often have to help our clients understand why the "uglier" text is a much better choice for certain platforms, and why they can't have their sleek and polished thin fonts with zippy-looking graphics instead. You must avoid making your content come off looking like a brand commercial. Nothing sends viewers running to the exits faster than something that feels like it's trying to sell you something.

An example of marrying text and images the right way is the "Stinky Fish Challenge" video we made in 2018 for Tubi TV, a free video-on-demand service supported by ads, which distributes on-line movies and TV shows produced by MGM, Paramount, and Lionsgate. Focusing on its slogan of "Free TV," Tubi wanted to draw attention to its service by giving people something of value: a free TV.

For the first video, we dreamed up an extreme challenge that would grab people's attention. In it, an interviewer walks up to people on the street and tells them that they can have a free TV if they complete one simple task: eating two bites of the stinkiest fish on earth. The fish is a canned product from Sweden that smells like herring that's been fermenting inside a latrine for months on end, and tastes even worse (or so I'm told).

The video starts with visually engaging shots of the cans being opened and a gross-looking substance being revealed, while a bold headline blinks on the top of the video, screaming, "STINK ALERT! THIS IS THE STINKIEST FISH ON EARTH!" We then cut to real people attempting to eat the fish and having terrible reactions, including one guy who grabs a bucket and looks like he's about to . . . All right, now I am hooked! *

---

* "Stinky Fish Challenge" aired via Tubi TV August 4, 2018.

Watching people opening the cans, you can practically smell how bad the fish mixture is by how they react. This all takes about 8 seconds, and then, once the viewer is engaged, the host comes on and actually explains the challenge and the video rolls. This is a great example of how you marry the text and visuals.

With some videos, you won't have the luxury of compelling visuals, like opening cans of stinky fish. Longer, more thoughtful videos can create a challenge in engaging the viewer and getting them hooked. A secret weapon you can use in these cases is the meme box. A meme is defined as a cultural symbol or social idea that is transmitted virally. You see some version of it online everyday. If you're not familiar with it, a "meme box" is the actual box that surrounds a video, which can include bold text or imagery. This meme box can be effective in grabbing someone's attention because it offers a place to put a headline that immediately frames what the video is about.

We actually consider these meme boxes at the very start of our process, all the way back in ideation. For example, we created a campaign intended to play like a short film for one of our clients and because we knew that the cinematic quality of the content was important, there was no real way to create a super-captivating opening. By adding a meme text that placed the entire piece in a captivating context, we were able to not only get viewers past that hump but also get them to understand where the entire story was coming from and frame them up to be emotionally receptive.

Influencers like Jay Shetty and Prince Ea are digital kings of the meme box and use the format like seasoned pros. If you look at their most successful videos, you'll see that many of them include a meme box that provides clear and compelling copy on who the video is intended for and why you should watch it. For example, if you scroll through Jay's videos, you'll find a treasure-trove of wisdom that is relatable and helpful for real people. His meme-box titles include "If You've Just Broken Up, Watch This" — and if you've just broken up with your girlfriend, then you're definitely going to give this one a look. Or "How Gratitude Can Change Your Life," or my personal favorite — "Before You Feel Pressure, Watch This." If you're going through a stressful time, this is going to grab your full attention. These titles present a clear value proposition for the viewer. They are easy to understand and they are specific. Learn from Jay, he is the master. And keep experimenting until you find a meme that people respond to.

3. It's All About the First 7 Seconds

As discussed in detail earlier, the beginning of your video is everything. When people are scrolling through their social media feed, they make split-second decisions as to what to stop and pay attention to. If something relatable or interesting catches their eye, they will stop and click on it. If they are not instantly drawn in, they are quickly on to the next thing and likely gone forever.

At Shareability, we spend a crazy amount of time thinking about the first 7 seconds. It has become our obsession. Having been in-volved in hundreds of videos, we know that the first 7 seconds is everything. You could have the most amazing story, one worthy of an Oscar or the viral Hall of Fame, but if you don't draw your audience in during those first 7 seconds, they will never see it.

We've learned this the hard way. I talked earlier about our video "Snowboarding In The Clouds," which took way too long to get to, well, snowboarding in the clouds.

Another painful example is an epic music video that we created for Cricket Wireless called "Make a Deal." The concept was sim-ple — create a catchy mock music video that glorifies the "thrifty ones," that is, people that know how to get a great deal. The inter-net loves a good deal, the memes and success stories around being thrifty run deep across the web, and this campaign gave us the per-fect opportunity to have fun with this dynamic. We created a killer music video that played right into the sweet spot of the internet, celebrating those crafty enough to pay less than the average sucker.

The song had a great hook and included verses like this — "Packed snacks. Bargain racks. Crossed state lines for the sales tax. But still those prices whack. So grab your secret stash . . . of coupons! So ev-erybody knows . . . you just made a deal!!" It was shot like an epic music video, with numerous locations and epic background danc-ers. When we screened it for the company, the video got a great re-sponse, and I expected that it would add another viral trophy to our digital mantel.

But then we made a mistake.

Because it was a music video, our team thought it was import-ant to try to get people to turn the sound on in the beginning of the video. So we created a version that added a 3, 2, 1 countdown to the start, where we tried to tell viewers to turn the sound on. After 8 seconds of that, we cut to a static shot of an exterior of a grocery store for 2 seconds. By the time our hip-hop artist came on screen and said "Let's do it," it had already been 10 seconds. By that point, everyone online was gone.

Because we were under a compressed timeline on the project, *we didn't have the time to test it.* Our normal testing process would have surely uncovered the problem, but without that step we were left to our own best judgment, which turned out not to be very good this time.

The video went out on social media with a 10-second intro that provided no value to the viewer whatsoever. And as a result, it landed with a thud. Out of 13 campaigns that we have executed for Cricket Wireless to date, "Make a Deal" has been the least successful in terms of views and engagement. All because we messed up the first 7 seconds.

On the other hand, a positive example of nailing the intro is a video that we worked on with British comedian Seann Walsh. Standup comedy can be a tough match for social media platforms, as a guy or girl talking into a microphone is not exactly the most at-tention-grabbing visual. And think about somebody watching with the sound off. Even if they stuck around for 7 seconds, it would be really hard for them to gauge whether or not the opening was actu-ally funny.

Seann was having challenges getting people to watch clips of his new standup routine. Then he had a genius idea. He decided to act out the scenes that he was describing in his comedy routine in or-der to put a funny visual gag to his jokes; in short, he was taking the video from audio comedy and making it visual comedy. He then picked a universally relatable subject — the fact that technology (mo-bile phones, social media, etc.) is changing friendships and how we interact. The video played as a narrated short film about the chal-lenges of hanging out with your friend in the internet era. We helped him with the packaging, putting the video in a meme box that read "How technology has changed the way you hang out with friends."

The text was simple, easy to understand, and relatable as a topic that most people have faced. It drew people in and got a lot more viewers to then turn on the sound and give his comedy a chance. You should check it out as well — the video is hilarious.

Testing . . . One, Two, Three

Now that you understand the principles, it's time to get into testing. For the purposes of this book, I'm going to break down the testing process into three different levels. I've adopted these levels from the philosophy of how we test our content, but as most of you don't have a social analytics team like we do, I have simplified the levels so that the information is usable for most brands and personalities. The first level is free and only requires your time and a keen eye. The second two have varying costs, but they can provide invaluable feedback and are well worth budgeting for. They will pay for themselves many times over through increased organic reach and media efficiencies as you move on to distribute to a wider audience.

Level One: The Backwards Test

I'll spend the most time on this level because it's free to execute and because it might be the most useful to those of you without a marketing agency at your disposal. The curious thing about this first level of testing is that it doesn't involve any actual testing. I call it the Backwards Test because it involves looking backwards and studying as many relevant variables from the past as you can get your hands on. Or, said in another way, you're doing research on yourself and others and seeing what's worked in the past instead of looking to what you think might work in the future (hence, we call it backwards).

This research takes the form of three different buckets.

BUCKET 1: BACKWARDS TESTING

The first bucket relates to any content that you or your brand has posted previously on any of your social media platforms. This tends to be the most relevant and useful information. The first step is to methodically review and catalog all of the posts that you've made to date. Separate them by platform (YouTube, Instagram, Facebook, etc.) and then put them in a spreadsheet with the date, the type of post (video versus photo versus third-party content), time of post, number of views or impressions, and number of Likes, comments, or shares, and so on. The details will vary by platform, but the essence is always the same.

You need to also factor in your own subscriber growth. Assuming you have had some growth, more people have been exposed to your more recent posts because you have more subscribers than you did when you posted a year earlier, for example. If you want to go to the next step of analysis, and I *highly* recommend that you do so, you can create a column called "engagement rate." We've talked about this before, and to us this is one of the key metrics of performance.

We look at engagement rate for everything that we do because it is the great equalizer and allows us to compare videos that would otherwise be apples to oranges. To recap, the way this works is pretty straightforward: the engagement rate is the percentage of people who watched a video and then liked, shared, or commented on the post. To calculate the engagement rate, you simply add up all of the engagements (Likes, shares, comments) and then divide that number by the total number of views. An example: if you had 100 engagements on 10,000 views, then 100/10,000 = 0.01. Then just move the decimal point two spots to the right and you have the engagement rate percentage, in this case, 1 percent. If you have 1,500 engagements on 300,000 views, then 1,500/300,000 = 0.005, or 0.5

percent. We've found that in the brand world, typical engagement rates are very poor, with most brands in the range of 0.1 to 0.2 percent; 5 percent is an outlier in the brand world, and 1 percent is, as you should know by now, the gold standard.

If you're a personality or influencer, the engagement percentage can be much higher, especially in the early days; when your subscriber numbers are low, your engagement rate can be inflated by supportive family and friends. Maintaining that high engagement rate as you scale is the hard part. Some of Jay Shetty's videos can exceed 4–5 percent while racking up millions of views. That is the dream.

Now that you have the data clearly spelled out, spend some substantial time poring over all of the entries with a critical eye, and see what you can learn. If you're an individual posting photos, maybe you'll find that your family likes engaging with pictures of you being active in nature, while your close friends love seeing you dressed up and getting rowdy on a night on the town. If you're a brand, you may find that any post regarding a product offer has extremely low engagement, but when you post about the community service that your company is involved in, the numbers are much higher.

This leads to a whole host of questions that can inform and direct your future content decisions. What type of content gets the best reaction? What format gets the most response? Is it videos, photos, or third-party content? Does the time of your post affect engagement? Is it better for you to post in the morning, around midday, or in the evening? How about the day of the week? Do your most successful posts have something in common? Do your least effective posts have something in common? Are there posts that had low viewership but a high engagement rate, or vice versa? What are the elements of your brand or personality that people seem to relate to? Do you need to go back and adjust what makes you shareable?

Ask as many questions as you can come up with, and look at the numbers from all angles. It sounds very simple, but curiously, most people don't take the time to go through this exercise and then think critically about what makes their content resonate. Just this one step alone can give you a big head start on your competition.

BUCKET 2: COMPETITOR ANALYSIS

Speaking of your competition, the second bucket refers to anyone that you consider a competitor to what you're doing or what you want to build. If you're building a brand in the skin-care space, for example, do an informal audit of all of the brands that you find relevant in your space. One way to do this is to research the main social media accounts of the brands that you want to learn from. Go through their YouTube, Instagram, and Facebook accounts, and find their ten best-performing posts from each, then put the results from these posts into a spreadsheet like the one you used for your own content.

Once you have that information, you can use the following questions to learn as much as you can and spot patterns. Overall, how is the quality of content in the space? Which brands have been most effective? Which brands have been least effective? Of the effective brands, is there a consistent theme or voice to their content? What topics are resonating with their audience? Which topics are getting the lowest response? Is there a format that is consistently performing the best? Are videos working better than photos on certain platforms? How often are they posting? Is there anything you can learn from the time of week and even the time of day the successful posts went live? What is the engagement rate of your competitors? What in the category as a whole is doing well? What in the category is not doing well? Where is the content opportunity that nobody is owning?

If you take the time to do this, it will give you invaluable feedback as to where the opportunity is and what audiences in your specific space are responding to. It will also help position you in relationship to your competition so you can carve out a niche.

BUCKET 3: DREAM BIG

The third bucket is the dream bucket. This entails all the brands or personalities that you aspire to become over time, your digital idols that are blazing the trail and having massive success with their social content. It's a great exercise to define who you admire in the space and who you dream to be, so that you can start to build the roadmap to get there.

As with the competitor bucket, I'd suggest choosing five to ten brands or personalities that you view as being highly successful with their content. Your list can include both brands and personalities, and they don't need to fall within the exact space that you are playing in. But they should include a few examples that have some level of industry relevance. Where this differs is in *the approach* to how you study them.

First, spend some time poring over all of their content. Take a look at their early posts, from back when they were just starting out on social media, and then compare those videos to what they are putting out now. What has changed? What have *they* learned, and how have they adjusted?

In most cases the early content will appear much less focused and "in the zone" than the current content. This is good news! Even your heroes took time to find out what they do best.

Now look at the top ten videos or posts for each of the examples, and also analyze the ten that had the *least* engagement. What jumps out at you between the two categories? What did they do right when their content succeeded? What do you think they did wrong when it didn't work?

After you've got a good feel for all of their content, ask the following questions: What makes each brand or personality special? What is their unique voice? How would you explain them to a friend, in one sentence? What topics do they cover? What trends are they riding? What value do they provide to their audience? Do they flip the script? How approachable or distant do they feel? What are they doing better than anyone else? What could they be doing even better?

Answer these questions and you'll be a big step closer to where you want to be.

Level Two: The Content Test

Once you have done all the soft testing you can, it's time to take a brave step into the real world — you need to test your content on a real audience.

This sounds scary, and many brands are very nervous about the idea of making something go live before they are completely satisfied with it, but it's a key part of success on social media.

Because the algorithms that control our social platforms are so vast, and their computing power so great, tapping into them early and running your content against them to see how it performs is absolutely crucial to ensuring success. This is especially true because those algorithms are the AI gatekeepers to your audience. *In short, if they don't like your content, either your audience won't see it or, best case, you will have to pay a premium for the privilege. For example, the cost of a view on Facebook for a traditional ad that is lower in the algorithm may be 6 to 8 cents. Meanwhile, the cost of a paid view for a shareable piece of content may be only 1 to 2 cents. That is a huge difference!*

To explain the importance of this, let me share another one of our spectacular failures. When creating a campaign for FitTea, the herbal supplement beverage to help an upset stomach, we decided to ride the wave of a big movie coming out, called *The Purge*. We were right to bank on this trend, as the movie franchise has proven hugely successful and spawned numerous sequels. We created a killer piece of content, a complete spoof of the trailer for *The Purge*, and designed to launch it days before Thanksgiving. The entire horror premise was built around the idea that people overeat during the holiday. Whereas in the movie, all crime is legal for 24 hours, in our trailer, all food was edible for 24 hours. People literally roamed the streets like zombies, looking for turkey feasts, breaking into stores, and raiding candy aisles with ravenous fervor. And the title was the real kicker. A direct play on the title *The Purge,* our fake movie was called *The Binge.*

Everything was perfect. Except the timeline. Not only did we not have time to do any tests, but the job was awarded so late that we finished the video hours before it was meant to launch. We didn't even have time to run it past the ad platforms to see if it passed . . .

It didn't.

The ad blockers thought that there was disturbing content in the video. There really wasn't — our "zombies" were just people eating turkey legs — but that didn't stop the automated visual programming from flagging it and forbidding any spend. Because it got flagged, the video got pushed down in the algorithm, and we had no way to put a single promotional dollar behind it. All of that glorious creative work we were all so proud of just launched weakly and languished. It launched from a relatively dead page, with very limited engagement or traction.

The original idea was that our campaign would change all that, that we would put some spend behind the content to kick-start it, and then the internet would do its thing. But without a push, it never gained any traction. The campaign lingered with hundreds of thousands of views instead of millions — all because we didn't have time to test it.

Now, we know better than to take on these tight turnarounds.

Whenever we can, we bake a two- to four-week testing period

into our work on any campaign. We then spend that time creating endless variations of the video and running them as "dark" posts, to see what resonates with certain audiences.

There are a lot of concepts to understand here. I'm not going to cover how to buy paid media on Facebook; if you're not familiar with it, there are countless articles on the web that can walk you through it. So let's start with the idea of "dark" posts. A dark post is something that you publish but that does not show up in your timeline. It's a setting within the Facebook ad platform, for example, where your post gets pushed to a real audience exactly the way a "real" or "live" post would, meaning it shows up in their feed and they interact with it exactly the way they normally would, but the difference is that it doesn't show up in your feed. That means that no one can search for it or find it by looking you up. The post is "dark" to anyone except for the people you are pushing it to.

So what do you test with dark posts? Well, trying out several different versions of the beginning of your video is a great place to start. You know the first 7 seconds is everything, so test different versions of that. Which opening image gets people's attention the most? What opening text copy makes more people go full screen? Does the color of the text matter? Does the animation in or around the text have an impact? What if you start the story at the end and create a teaser before you go into the real thing?

There are a million variables, and the key is finding those that truly matter to the story you are telling. This changes on every video, but it often connects to the very beginning.

That said, seeing how the data plays out over time is also very interesting. When we did our photo restoration project for Adobe, for example, we realized that even though a particular edit of the video tested slightly better for initial viewership, there was another version of the video that came in a close second on viewership but actually had slightly higher retention through the last quarter of the video. In particular it carried more people across the messaging at the very end, telling us that the desired impact of the video would actually be greater. In that case, we went with the second option.

It's also important to understand *what* you are actually testing for. While it may sound like you are testing for creative feedback, to see what people think of your content, and while that can be true, more often than not, you are really testing for what the algorithm likes. You are getting data back that says the algorithm will serve this particular piece to more people, or for a lower cost. That is all well and good, but you have to keep the effectiveness of your campaign in mind and remember the ultimate mission. It's easy to get lost in reaching for the most views every time, but at the end of the day, is that what truly matters? Probably not.

Level Three: The Audience Test

Now that you have your content honed, and you have a sense of what the algorithms like, it's time to focus on your audience.

The tools for segmenting your audience on these platforms are insanely sophisticated. You can divide people not just by basics, such as age, gender, ethnicity, and geographic location, but also by whether or not they like Alice Cooper, dogs, or bicycle pumps.

As part of our learning process we launched a channel called Like It GRL, which was geared squarely to teenage girls. It was an exercise in seeing how effective we could get with our targeting. We spent months tweaking details, not even video content but post copy, just to figure out what kind of language we needed to speak, to reach our desired demo. We learned things that may seem obvious and intuitive, such as teenage girls absolutely *love* emojis and generally don't want to read too much. Having the actual data to back this up gave us the confidence to make it a rule that our posts were to include massive amounts of emojis but no more than three to five words. Our audience skyrocketed and our costs went way down.

The way we do this with our bigger campaigns is very varied, but the philosophy is always consistent. We start by figuring out our ideal target audience. Sometimes this comes with great specificity from our clients, telling us they want to reach a very precise group of people, based on some much larger objective they have. They might be running a campaign for back to school, and they want to reach only married parents of two or more children in middle-class house-holds in the coastal regions, for example. Or an even more specific campaign, like our first video for mall company Macerich, asking us to focus our campaign for the King's Plaza Shopping Center in Brooklyn around the geographic region where the Town Center (Macerich-speak for "mall") was located. We drove a million views from within a few miles of that mall alone. If you know someone in Brooklyn, ask them if they have seen it. Odds are they have.

As you test your content, you will see that different iterations speak to different audience groups. This will teach you how to hone and refine not just your content, but also your audience. Perhaps there is some metric that is not hyper-relevant to your messaging but that will have a huge impact on your spend because the algo-rithm is much happier serving the content to that particular sub-group. Without testing, there is really no way of knowing.

Now, the cost.

Well, running the tests doesn't have to be very expensive at all. The amount of money you spend really only dictates two things: how many tests you can run — and how wide an audience they will reach.

The way this works is that you create anywhere from two to five different versions that you are looking to run against each other. Five is the maximum because past that, it gets really complicated to analyze and the variables are too great. You load them into your ad account, set the spend you are willing to put against them, and hit run. (Okay, that's an oversimplification, but essentially right.) The spend can be anywhere from a few dollars to a few hundred to a few thousand and up, but that's all you need. Even the smaller budgets will give you an audience size of thousands of people, certainly more than any TV focus group ever.

The trouble is time. Each iteration needs to run for at least two days. If you are testing 10 or 20 different versions, well, do the math . . .

At Shareability, we do all of this using software, but unless you have access to some costly subscription-based or proprietary software, this is a labor-intensive task. We might be able to do it in a few weeks, sometimes even a few days, but do not underestimate the effort involved. Learn from our mistakes and make sure you have enough time on your hands to run all the tests you can imagine.

A Final Note: With Paid Media, All Content Is Not Created Equal

When it comes to paid advertising on social media, all content is not created equal. On television, when a company runs a TV commercial on a Thursday night, that spot is priced based on the time slot. Taco Bell and Ford pay the same $800,000 to run a 30-second ad, and that ad receives roughly the same exposure, no matter what commercial they run. The internet is completely different, as advertising on all the major social platforms is auction-based, meaning the price is determined by how easy or difficult it is for the platform to serve the ad. And because social media is extremely targeted, you don't need millions of dollars to advertise. In fact you can start as low as a few dollars to see what results you initially get and then spend increasing amounts when you see that an ad is working. A few thousand dollars can have a big impact with a targeted demographic.

One of the most important features in determining this on Facebook, one that a surprising amount of people in the advertising world don't even know about, is the Facebook relevancy score. For every piece of promotable content uploaded to Facebook, the algorithm assigns a relevancy score of 1 (worst) to 10 (best) based on a number of factors. Most important is how viewable the algorithm considers the content to be, based on the engagement of the initial audience that views the videos. In truth, most advertisements provide little to no value to the audience and therefore have extremely low engagement, which in turn results in a low relevancy score, in the 1–4 range. Quality content that is marginally shareable falls into the middling 4–6 range. And highly shareable content, which receives substantial engagement, receives a relevancy score of 7–10. This score is everything when you are putting paid promotion behind your content. *Videos with high relevancy scores climb the algorithm, more people want to see the content, and Facebook in turn charges you less to push paid views.* On the opposite end, content with low relevancy scores drops down in the algorithm, making it harder for Facebook to distribute that content, and therefore the price goes through the roof.

By posting a brand video that drives substantial engagement, you receive a higher relevancy score and trigger the algorithm to push that video out to a larger audience at a much lower cost per view. Conversely, if your video receives minimal engagement, it will slide down in the algorithm and you will have to pay higher rates to push it out.

Let's say a cereal company runs a dull ad about the fiber content of its bran flakes. An ad with such minimal shareable value to the viewer will result in predictably low engagement rates, and therefore it will receive a relevancy score of 1 or 2. The lower relevancy score causes the Facebook algorithm to work harder to deliver the ad, and therefore Facebook needs to charge more to push it out. A score of 2 might mean that the cost of a view is in the range of 8–10 cents. Contrast that with one of our hero videos that is rapidly viewed, liked, and shared by hundreds of thousands, and consequently stamped with a relevancy score of 9. Because that video is being proactively viewed and shared, the Facebook algorithm actually becomes our ally and helps push it out to a broader audience and charges far less money to do it, sometimes at less than 1 cent per view.

This dynamic presents a huge opportunity for brands that are funneling their media budgets away from traditional media like television and into social and digital media where — if they follow the principles outlined in this book — they can break through the noise, drive massive attention, build deep relationships with customers online, and save millions of dollars in the process.

Epilogue

Finding Your Way
with the New Rules

I hope you enjoyed reading this book as much as I've enjoyed writing it. That's because this exercise provided me with an opportunity to take a breath and look back over my career, and to reflect on how much has changed. Over the past two decades, technology has changed the way in which human beings communicate, it has changed the way we interact with each other, and it has revolutionized the way in which we interact with brands and with new personalities on the rise. The digital revolution has disrupted virtually every brand category, from Uber to Netflix to Dollar Shave Club, and in addition, personalities and celebrities have come forth, all due to the unprecedented impact of social media. Any time there is disruption at this level, there is also a tremendous opportunity. An opportunity to embrace the amazing tools that digital gives you. An opportunity to use content and data to build relationships directly with your customers. An opportunity to build a brand that is more valuable than you ever thought was possible.

My favorite part of my job is noticing how fast everything changes. My partner Nick Reed and I often joke that we really don't want to leave the office at night because when we show up the next day, things will be different. We've found that when you actively embrace that kind of change, it can take you to some pretty fun places.

Looking back over the first three years of our company, we did a lot of crazy things, but we had never become involved in the music space. That all changed when we were introduced to the management team for Dua Lipa, an up-and-coming artist on Warner Bros. Records. Dua has a contemporary voice and talent in spades, as you are probably aware of by now. But when we were introduced to her in early 2017, her record label was still trying to figure out how to break her into the US market. At the time, she was popular in Europe and had a few successful collaborations with major artists, but was virtually unknown in America.

At the same time, we were talking to Hyatt hotels, which was looking to use music and social media to bring a young, hip vibe to their new brand, the Hyatt Unbound Collection.

A match was made. We collaborated with Dua Lipa's team on a strategy to produce an array of shareable content around Dua and her soon-to-be-released single "New Rules." Hyatt bankrolled all of the content, including the music video for "New Rules," helmed by the amazing UK director Henry Scholfield. Shareability also produced an array of social content around the production, featuring Dua and the making of the video, including two live performances. The entire campaign was backed by a substantial media spend.

For the shoot, we took over the Confidante Miami Beach, an updated 1950s art deco resort, which is owned by Hyatt. In the video, as the lyrics to the song go, Dua is pulled out of a funk by her girlfriends as she tries to forget about a worthless boyfriend and move on with her life. Her girlfriends give her a musical pep talk as they dance through the hotel and head out into the South Beach sunshine to take a cleansing swim in the hotel's pool, where flamingos are frolicking and mischief is on the horizon.

The "New Rules" video exploded online, quickly attaining unicorn status with more than 1 *billion* views. As it cut through the digital noise, so did Dua Lipa, who rocketed to superstardom. She became the first female artist since Adele to have a number-one hit in the UK, and she eventually went number one in the United States as well. Her Spotify streaming numbers, the new benchmark in the music business, increased by over 800 percent. Her popularity since then has only risen further, and she is one of the most played artists on traditional radio.

For Hyatt, the campaign became the most successful social media campaign that the company had ever been a part of, driving over 50 million views on their social channels, giving substantial heat, and building a cool factor around the Hyatt Unbound Collection brand.

Watching how quickly a previously unknown artist can ascend to the top of the music business is inspiring. It reminds us that in this new digital world, it can also happen for brands just as quickly.

Moving forward, a big focus for Shareability is not only helping existing brands navigate their own digital transformations, but using the power of digital to launch new ones.

A prime example of this is a brand called SAGE that we're helping get off the ground. SAGE is the brainchild of journalist Jessica Yellin, whose name you may recognize because she's a former senior correspondent for CNN. Yellin came to CNN in 2007 as a political reporter in the lead-up to the 2008 presidential election. At the time, the presumptive nominees were Hillary Clinton for the Democrats and John McCain for the Republicans, and those two individuals were heavily covered by the senior political correspondents at CNN. Since Yellin was relatively new, lacked seniority, and was, well, a woman, she was placed on a different beat, sent off to the Midwest to cover a relatively unknown senator from Illinois, Barack Obama.

As Obama's star rose, so did Yellin's. She followed him all the way to the White House, eventually becoming CNN's chief White House correspondent.

But for all of her success, Yellin was not happy. She had an inside look at how the news business operated, and even though she was contributing to it at the highest level, she didn't like it. She often speaks of the edict handed down to her to "make news more like ESPN," where color commentators were engaged in "heated and passionate debates" or, more accurately, yelling matches, over largely irrelevant topics. "News is about conflict," they would say. "Outrage wins viewers."

Whenever something important would be happening at the White House, perhaps an introduction of new policy that would affect millions of Americans, Yellin would pitch an intelligent and thoughtful story that could get the facts out to the viewers in a calm and informed way, only to be told time and time again that this was too "dry" or "boring" and to focus instead on covering the White House reactions to the Obama birth certificate "scandal" or the placement of the White House Christmas tree ornaments.

The news business was becoming so commoditized that sensationalism was not just seeping but flooding into all the established networks. Even CNN, a network once considered a bastion of serious and breaking news, was becoming a loud and flashing mess of attention-hoarding infotainment — all with the pressing and short-term goal of driving ratings to satisfy advertisers.

The end result of all this, of course, is that the news business as a whole is suffering. They are losing viewers in droves as people are running away from the loud, bombastic, constant bombardment of "breaking news" every time there is a cat up a tree, and instead are turning to the safe cocoon of their social media feeds. Yellin is looking to change all of that.

After she left CNN, she took some time off to contemplate her future. She thought about her experiences in the news business and the path of news reporting in general. She watched the news from an outside perspective for the first time and recognized a singular truth that had somehow escaped her when she was battling from the inside — *where were all the women?*

Every single newsroom she had ever been a part of was always run by men. This was somehow just the tradition and an accepted truth. Women were relegated to being on-camera talent because they were "prettier to look at." Yellin herself was constantly receiving feedback from the newsroom on her on-camera performance, not based on the substance of her reporting but on the way her hair would move in the wind. "Why does your hair have to move?" Well, because she was outside and the damned wind was blowing. What does this have to do with news?

Absolutely nothing.

Yellin started asking questions, specifically looking for feedback from women from all walks of life. What did they think of the news? Did they watch it? What did they like? What did they not like?

As it turned out, news makes women feel lied to, nervous, and anxious. As a result, they don't watch it. The whole edict of "conflict and outrage" was not working on half the population.

This was a staggering revelation. Yellin dug deeper, springing for a real study in partnership with leading educational institutions. It turned out her anecdotal research was spot on. Seventy-four percent of women are currently "taking a break" from news. Sixty-eight percent say they get an anxiety hangover from watching. Only an abysmal 23 percent say they feel in any way informed by watching the news.

Women wanted news that gave them facts, not opinions, and news that was informative, not repetitive. They want things explained — if taxes are up or down, how does that affect not just their life but also others, and what does it *mean?* They also need to find out about all of this quickly and calmly so they can move on with their lives.

Yellin saw the need for a female-led newsroom delivering video news directly to your social media feed. She would need to build a team of Emmy and Peabody Award–winning journalists, investigative reporters, experts in finance, immigration, women's issues, science, entertainment, culture, and of course, politics.

The news media is currently a $120 billion business, and that's without women watching. If news could capture women viewers, that figure could balloon to $200 billion. That's an $80 billion market gap waiting for someone to claim it.

Yellin is stepping up by creating SAGE. Will her effort gain traction and become the next great voice in American news? Only time will tell. But it sure is fun to be in the trenches, trying to disrupt a national institution that really hasn't successfully adapted to the internet age.

Another project that we're working on is a skin-care brand launching in partnership with a major music star. The genesis of this brand is a conversation that I had with a major e-commerce company, where they shared data showing how skin-care-product sales are growing rapidly with Generation Z. Can you guess the reason? I'll give you a hint — it has everything to do with this book. If you haven't guessed it by now, the reason is social media.

The average 20-year-old girl today takes more pictures in a day than her mom took in a year. That's a pretty crazy stat, but it's totally consistent with what we see. And because of all of these close-ups for Instagram, adolescents and young adults are paying far more attention to their skin. And hence, skin-care products are on the rise.

So we're launching a new brand that was built from the ground up for the selfie generation. It will include all of the skin and facial products you need to look your best, all wrapped in a positivity brand with the soul and aesthetic of Generation Z. As you might expect, we're launching the brand exclusively on digital, without any traditional brick-and-mortar retailers, in partnership with an e-commerce behemoth. To launch the brand, we're going to create a tidal wave of promotion and positivity around the brand, with a music artist pushing to their tens of millions of fans on social media, from Facebook, YouTube, and Instagram to our e-commerce partner driving search and promotion on their platform. Soon after this book is out, the brand will be in the market, and if we've done our job right, you will know exactly which one it is. I can't wait to see what you think.

Since Shareability was first founded, the only constant has been our ability to make changes and constantly start over. My message to you is that you should also keep your eye open for this kind of opportunity in your area of interest and for your brand, no matter its size, as opportunities yet to be discovered abound.

Because everything in the internet world is rapidly advancing, you need to be in a state of continuous evolution. Remember to always keep learning from those who are having success and constantly be studying what's happening on social media platforms, from social media stars like Jay Shetty to innovative brands like Dollar Shave Club to the script-flippers like Poppy.

Staying ahead of the internet zeitgeist is a challenge and a nonstop process of constant iteration, but with the tools you have from this book, you are well prepared to meet that challenge. At Shareability, we work hard to stay on the edge of innovation, which keeps our energy level high. As one of our advisors proudly said about us, "Shareability is always skating to where the puck is going to be, as opposed to where it is." I hope this book will help you do the same.

ACKNOWLEDGMENTS

To my co-author Josh Young — you rock. It is rare to find someone with so much talent combined with so much grace. Thank you for everything you've done in making this book happen and for putting up with my quirks and missed deadlines. It has been an absolute blast to work together.

To my publisher Rick Wolff at Houghton Mifflin, it has truly been a dream to work with you. You took a risk on this book and I will forever be grateful. Thank you to Rosemary McGuinness for keeping us on track and making things go smoothly, and to Brooke Borneman, Sari Kamin, and the entire publicity and marketing team for your genius and support.

To my brilliant partner Nick Reed, who cofounded Shareability and brought Josh and me together to write this book — thank you for all that you do. This book and this company wouldn't have happened without you.

To the crazy Swede Joel Bergvall, you are an amazing partner who helped tremendously in bringing this book to life. Whether it is creative concepts, video scripts, book drafts, or poker games — anything you touch only gets better. A lot better. You are the man.

To the calm in the storm, my partner Erick Brownstein, you are the man that makes it all happen. Thank you for everything that you've done in building this company and giving it heart. I can't wait to see what comes next.

To my friend of twenty years and new partner Mike Allen, thank you for joining us on this journey. I've seen the success you've had at the highest levels of brands and agencies and have long dreamed about working together. We are honored and excited to have you on board.

To our new chairman Jean-Yves Charlier, thank you for believing in us and for pushing us out of our comfort zone. Your insights and relationships have already been invaluable in taking this company to the next level.

To Patrick Mazuca at Shareability for your insights on the book and fantastic analogy of the internet city. Great stuff!

To our investors at Bunim Murray, we couldn't be more excited about being in business with you. Jonathan Murray and Gil Gold-schein, you have built an amazing company at the intersection of content and pop culture. Jonathan Stern, thank you for believing in us and for making our partnership happen.

To the entire team at Shareability, thank you for everything that you do. I am consistently blown away by your talents and what you are able to make happen. I am even more impressed by what good people you are. Big things are ahead!

To my literary agent Andrew Stuart, thank you for helping shape the concept and for pushing the project along both creatively and on the business front.

To my friend and teacher Dr. John Kim: I showed up in your office one day a stressed out, beaten man and had no idea that my life was about to completely change. Thank you for everything that you do for me and for the team at Shareability. You are an amazing talent and there is not a person in the world that would not be better off for knowing you.

To my friend and partner Michael Redd, you are the man. I am inspired by your talent but blown away by your humility. It has been an absolute pleasure to spend time together and to get to know you and Achea.

To my good friend Matt Hickenbotham, who left us way too soon: They say that the candle that burns twice as bright burns half as long, and no one was as bright as you. I miss you buddy.

To my awesome and beautiful wife, Darcy, thank you for supporting me through this crazy entrepreneurial journey. Though all the stressful nights and weekends behind a laptop you always had my back and brought positivity. My life is so much better because I met you.

To my amazing kids Max and Allie, thank you for putting up with me through all of the weekends I was behind a laptop writing this book. Now let's go have some fun!

To my brothers Andy and Jay, it has been quite the ride from Plainview Pkwy to Dallas, Phoenix, and L.A. Rufus would be proud.

To my mom and dad, Jim and Darlene Staples, thank you for everything that you have done for me. You've had a much bigger impact than you know.

Tim Staples

February 2019

INDEX

ABOUT THE AUTHORS

TIM STAPLES is an entrepreneur at the intersection of Hollywood and Silicon Valley. He is the cofounder and CEO of Shareability, a digital marketing company that uses content, data, and technology to drive explosive growth for major brands including Pepsi, AT&T, Hyatt, Adobe, and the Olympic Games. Prior to Shareability, Tim founded Converge, a digital marketing company that created content and promotional platforms with over a hundred major celebrities, including Rihanna, Victoria Beckham, 50 Cent, Shaquille O'Neal, Miley Cyrus, and Usher. Previously, he served as managing director of integration for Omnicom's The Marketing Arm, where he advised major brands on their strategy in sports and entertainment. Hollywood's TheWrap has named him one of the "Innovators Who Are Disrupting Hollywood."

JOSH YOUNG is a best-selling author whose work spans entertainment, science, law, natural history, business, politics, and sports. He has co-written 21 books, including 5 *New York Times* bestsellers, 2 additional *Los Angeles Times* bestsellers, 3 books that were made into TV documentaries, 15 books that have been ranked number one in their category on amazon.com, as well as 2 novels. Previously, he was a contributing editor at *George* magazine, a contributing writer to the *New York Times* and *Esquire,* and the host of *Screening Room* on the Discovery Times Channel.